The Lesser Existences

The Lesser Existences

Étienne Souriau,
an Aesthetics
for the
Virtual

A Univocal Book

Translated
by
Erik
Beranek

David Lapoujade

University of Minnesota Press
Minneapolis
London

The University of Minnesota Press gratefully acknowledges financial support for the publication of this book from the Centre national du livre.

Originally published in French as *Les Existences moindres*. Copyright 2017 by Les Editions de Minuit, 7, rue Bernard-Palissy, 75006 Paris.

"Art and Philosophy" was originally published in French as "Art et Philosophie," *Revue Philosophique de la France et de l'Etranger* (1954): 1–21. Copyright PUF/Humensis, 1954.

Translation copyright 2021 by the Regents of the University of Minnesota

Published by the University of Minnesota Press
111 Third Avenue South, Suite 290
Minneapolis, MN 55401-2520
http://www.upress.umn.edu

ISBN 978-1-5179-0465-4 (pb)

Library of Congress record available at https://lccn.loc.gov/2021005163

Printed in the United States of America on acid-free paper

The University of Minnesota is an equal-opportunity educator and employer.

30 29 28 27 26 25 24 23 22 21   10 9 8 7 6 5 4 3 2 1

Contents

Abbreviations

AA   *Avoir une âme, essai sur les existences virtuelles,* Société d'Édition *Les Belles Lettres,* 1938.

DME   *The Different Modes of Existence,* Univocal Publishing, 2015. This volume includes *The Different Modes of Existence* and Souriau's essay "Of the Mode of Existence of the Work-to-Be-Made" (both translated by Erik Beranek), as well as "The Sphinx of the Work" by Isabelle Stengers and Bruno Latour (translated by Tim Howles).

IP   *L'Instauration philosophique,* Librairie Félix Alcan, 1939.

OD   *L'Ombre de Dieu,* Presses universitaires de France, 1955.

1

One Monad Too Many?

It's February 21, 1930. Like on any other day, the man of many heteronyms, Fernando Pessoa, is walking the streets of Lisbon with his hat on his head and his fine-framed glasses perched on his nose. Like on any other day, he is tired, weary. He feels cut off from the external world and experiences the emptiness of his own existence. Generally speaking, he has the sense that, in his case, a "metaphysical mistake" was made.[1] One could say that he sees himself as being one monad too many. We know that, in the Leibnizian system, monads have neither doors nor windows: they have no need for any such openings to the external world, since the world is included in them in the form of various, ordered perceptions. Yet Pessoa's whole problem is that while he has perceptions, they don't allow him to experience the reality of the external world any more than the reality of his own existence. It's no longer reality that is external; rather, he's the one who is external to all reality. He's like a monad, but a worldless monad, shut in behind doors and windows. "A tenuous pane of glass stands between me and life. However clearly I see and understand life, I cannot touch it."[2] He is somehow deprived of the possibility of existing, though he still has to bear the weight of existence. If there is a "metaphysical error" here, it's that in creating the world, God never granted a place to this indecisive, dreamy, inactive monad with no connection to the real world.

1

But instead of continuing his stroll, halfway across a bridge, he suddenly stops.

> Suddenly, as if destiny had turned surgeon and, with dramatic success, operated on an ancient blindness, I raise my eyes from my anonymous life to the clear knowledge of the manner of my existence. . . . It is so difficult to describe the feeling one has when one feels that one really does exist and that the soul is a real entity, that I do not know what human words I can use to define it. . . . For many years—from the time I was born and became a conscious being—I too was someone else and now I wake up suddenly to find myself standing in the middle of the bridge, looking out over the river, knowing more positively now than at any moment before that I exist. But I do not know the city, the streets are new to me and the sickness incurable. So, leaning on the bridge, I wait for the truth to pass so that I can regain my null and fictitious, intelligent and natural self. It lasted only a moment and has passed now.[3]

What happened? All of a sudden the Pessoa monad was overwhelmed by the feeling of really existing, of being included in the world again, of being involved in it. "To know oneself precipitately, as I did in that moment of pure enlightenment, is suddenly to grasp Leibniz's notion of the dominant monad, the magic password to the soul."[4] Very quickly, however, he returns to his old certainties. He knows that he doesn't exist, that he never existed, and that he'll never again exist with such assurance as he did in that one moment. Once again, existence appears to him to be insignificant, unreal. Rather than assuring the thinker of his existence, as in Descartes, here thought confirms, on the contrary, that he does not exist, that he cannot exist. "I am surprised by everything I have been and that I now see I am not."[5] We clearly see the objection that might be raised against those who affirm their own nonexistence: they must exist if they're there to pose the question, they must be caught up in false problems. They seek a way into existence when their feet are already firmly planted in it. The whole problem is clearly absurd: how could you doubt the reality of existence when, in order to doubt it, you have to be a part of it, present in the world? And yet, the absurdity of the problem results from the confusion of two notions: existence and reality. From one perspective, this man really does exist: he occupies a given space-time, he is present among things, he crosses paths with passersby on the bridge, he gathers impressions, thoughts cross his mind. However, none of that is exactly real. The beings and things exist, but they lack reality. What does it mean to say that they "lack" reality? What could an existence possibly be lacking that would make it more real?

But aren't there existences that become "more" real, in the sense that they gain in strength, extension, or consistency: a love that deepens, a sorrow that heightens, a rage that swells? Or a plan that is realized, the construction of a building, the filming of a screenplay, the performance of a musical score? These are all ways of gaining in reality, of acquiring a greater presence, a more vivid radiance. The two series of examples aren't situated on the same plane, but they bear witness to similar processes. In the first series, we're dealing with beings that intensify the reality of their existence while remaining on the same plane. The beings in the second series, on the other hand, have to change their plane of existence in order for their reality to grow: they are possibles or virtuals, at first, and then they change their manner of being in order to become more real. In every case, the general problem is the same: how to make what exists more real?

The philosopher Étienne Souriau never stopped posing this question, as much in the domain of the arts as in that of philosophy or of individual existences. Who is Étienne Souriau (1892–1979)? Even though his rediscovery today rests largely on other aspects of his work, the memory of Souriau's name remains associated with the philosophy of art more than anything else. It is fairly well known that he oversaw the production of the sizable *Vocabulaire d'esthétique*, that he was professor of aesthetics at the Sorbonne, and that for many years he edited the *Revue d'esthétique*. Less known is the fact that he wrote works of pure philosophy like *Avoir une âme, essai sur les existences virtuelles* (1938), *L'Instauration philosophique* (1939), *Les Différents modes d'existence* (1943), and *L'Ombre de Dieu* (1955).[6] Does this mean that after these works Souriau lost interest in such questions and returned to aesthetics properly speaking? That, little by little, these investigations ceased to interest him, having never received a sufficient response? On the contrary, the texts devoted to souls, ontology, the definition of philosophy, God, or virtual realities must themselves be understood *as parts of a philosophy of art*. The entirety of Souriau's thought is a philosophy of art and never sought to be anything else.

This is one of the profoundly original aspects of his thought: aesthetics no longer plays a secondary or occasional role in philosophy, it is no longer a mere domain or area of philosophy, as when we speak of Hegel's or Schelling's aesthetics. Instead, it is the whole of philosophy that is subject to a superior aesthetics, to a dimension that, in *L'Instauration philosophique*, is identified as a "philosophy of philosophy." Before we can speak of the philosophy of art, we must speak of an art of philosophy itself—and not just as a figure of speech. We must imagine an art by which each philosophy posits or instaurs itself, before it can be applied to some determinate field.[7] Likewise, prior to any ontology of art, there must be an art of ontology, since there's no Being without some manner of being. We can only reach Being through the manners in which it is given. That is the theme of Souriau's work entitled *The Different Modes of Existence*. The art of Being is the infinite variety of its manners of being or modes of existence.[8] Whether we are dealing with texts devoted to souls, to existences, to philosophies, or to God, the aim is essentially the same. Souriau's oeuvre displays a magnificent coherence in this respect. Psychology, epistemology, ontology, and philosophy are resources for a profound philosophy of art.

What are we to make of this reversal? To understand it, we'll have to start from the "existential pluralism" with which Souriau himself begins. The first assertion of this pluralism is precisely that there isn't a single mode of existence for all the beings that populate the world, any more than there is a single world for all those beings. We don't exhaust the extent of the world by covering "all that exists according to one of its modes (for example, that of physical or psychical existence)" (DME, 101). Souriau lays out and examines the various modes of existence ranged between being and nothingness. Hamlet's mode of existence isn't the same as that of a square root, an electron's mode of existence isn't the same as that of a table, etc. They all exist, but each in its own manner. Conversely, a being isn't necessarily destined for a single mode of existence; it can exist according to several modes, and not just as a physical or mental entity: it can exist as a spiritual entity, as a value, as a representation, etc. This is Eddington's famous parable of the two tables, at once a solid presence and a cloud of electrons. Or Hamlet, who exists as a character in Shakespeare, as a presence on the stage, as a reference in a lecture, as the hero of a film, etc. A being can see its existence doubled, tripled—in short, it can exist on several, distinct planes, all while remaining numerically one.

One might object that the distinction is merely verbal, since this being actually *is* numerically one. But being numerically one, possessing unity and permanence in the manner of a thing, is itself only one mode of existence among others. A being can participate in several *planes of existence* as if it belonged to several worlds. An individual exists in this world: she exists in it as a body, she exists in it as a "psyche," but she also exists in it as a reflection in a mirror, as a motif, an idea, or a memory in someone else's mind—and all of these are different manners of existing, on different planes. In this sense, beings are plurimodal, multimodal realities; and what we call the world is actually the site of various "interworlds," of an entanglement of planes.

Now, each of these modes must be regarded as a distinct art of existing. That's why it's so interesting to take modes themselves as the starting point for thought. The mode is not an existence but a manner of making a being exist on one plane or another. It is a *gesture.* Each existence proceeds from a gesture that instaurs it, from an "arabesque" that determines it to be such as it is. This gesture doesn't issue from some creator but is immanent to the existence itself. From this point of view, "mode" and "manner" don't quite designate the same thing. Pushing the distinction, we can say that the mode (from *modus*) thinks existence on the basis of the limits or the measure of beings (as can be seen in the derivative term "moderation"), while the manner (from *manus*) thinks existence on the basis of the gesture, of the form that beings take when they appear. The mode limits a power of existing, while the manner reveals its singular form, line, and curve and thereby bears witness to an "art."[9]

If Souriau's philosophy is a philosophy of art, it isn't because he's concerned with forms but because he's concerned with the formal principle that organizes forms. Here, too, it is necessary to introduce a distinction and not to confuse "the form" with "the formal" (no more than we confuse "to form" with "to formalize"). The *form* is inseparable from a matter that it informs, drawing its boundaries or regulating its becoming as an end or entelechy. But the *formal* is what organizes the forms, what structures their relations architectonically. Generally speaking, we can say that the form is the principle of the organization of matters, while the formal is the principle of the structuration of forms.

This formal principle reveals itself through the particular radiance that gives certain moments of existence their splendor. Souriau loves to describe those moments in which existences are fully accomplished, in which they deploy an architectonic that installs them in their proper perfection, sublime moment, or utmost hour. "Those ochre peaks with mauve shadows; that blue sea. . . . What more could one ask for? This symphony is played entirely for its own sake. . . . Is it not completely perfect all the same? . . . In some sense, splendors of this sort are the good works of being, of pure art. Things in themselves, since they no longer lack anything at all."[10] It isn't only the good works of being or "pure art" that are subject to an art of existing but all existences, just as philosophy itself is subject to a superior art. We might suppose that Souriau's existential pluralism finds its model in the plurality of the arts (music, architecture, painting . . .). But in reality the opposite is the case: it is the arts that obtain their plurality from the diversity of manners of making a being exist, of promoting an existence or of rendering it real.[11]

We could, without a doubt, lead all the manners of being

back toward the ground[12] from which they all originate—Being—and identify philosophy with a fundamental ontology. But we could also follow this path in the opposite direction: we could examine the variety of different manners of being for their own sakes and make philosophy itself an exploration of manners of being. In that case, it's no longer a question of leading the modes toward a grounding (or toward a groundlessness more profound than any grounding)[13] but of studying the manner in which the modes rise up from the ground, the manner in which they depart from Being "as the sword's tip departs from the sword."[14] Sometimes the manners are manners of *being* and refer to a fundamental ontology; sometimes the manners are *manners* of being and refer to a modal or mannerist ontology.

Souriau distances himself from all fundamental ontology because he finds it always tends toward the false plenitude of the undetermined *(bathos)*, a plenitude that "seems to make all life swell with a prodigious enrichment" but is really only an illusion. This is a world "not only of darkness but also of vagueness and nothingness, from out of which sketches begin to take shape formally but also to blur and overlap with one another" (AA, 42). Souriau isn't interested in this indistinct ground but in the modes whose outlines begin to emerge from it, and which lay claim to their reality little by little as they gradually take shape and gain in determination. Most of these modes will never get beyond the state of being a sketch or a rough draft; they will never succeed in differentiating themselves from the indistinct base into which they will once again descend. But others will rise up toward their summits through an intensification of their reality. They will continue to gain in precision and "lucidity" until they reach their maximum. They are like thrusts of reality. Only such summits interest Souriau; he even goes so far as to imagine a universal accomplishment, "a universe that has arrived, peripherally, in all of its points, at the zone of integral accomplishment and of the lucent radiance of being" (AA, 43).

Each of Souriau's principal works explores a specific plurality: a plurality of souls in *Avoir une âme,* a plurality of modes of existence in *The Different Modes of Existence,* a plurality of "philosophemes" or philosophical systems in *L'Instauration philosophique*. In each case, Souriau begins with a *pluriverse* and posits a plurality of arts of existing—not with a universe, a diversity of sensible facts, or anything else that would pertain solely to a singular art (most often, the art of constituting objects of knowledge).[15] We might think that Souriau's aim is to propose a classification or to index the elements of these pluralities, and he does sometimes express himself as if this were the case. Thus, in *Avoir une âme*, Souriau distinguishes between souls that exist through representation (the idea we have of another when we attribute a soul to her, or the idea we have of ourselves in relation to the idea of ourselves that we attribute to another), souls that exist through ambition (the desire for self-expansion), souls that exist through illusion (the dream of an existence that is never accomplished), and souls that exist through possession (self-possession as the accomplishment of oneself, or possession of another through appropriation), and so on. And there's no doubt that a single soul can pass through several of these modes, becoming a transmodal being through however many internal revolutions or intensive variations.

Likewise, in *The Different Modes of Existence*, Souriau distinguishes between various modes of existence, which he treats as so many "elements" or "existential semantemes": from the radiant presence of the phenomenon all the way to the nearly nonexistent virtuals. There, too, everything is described in relation to a fundamental art of existing. The phenomenon has its way of positing itself with a perfection all its own; it has a manner of making itself apparent that constitutes its art of existing. "This art is the law of the phenomenon's radiance, the soul of its presence and its existential patuity," writes Souriau (DME, 138).[16] Its art reveals itself through the instantaneous architectonic that it unfolds in the sublimity of an instant. There is a "soul" of the phenomenon, which is like its signature or its unique tonality, as when we speak of the soul of a landscape. A completely different manner of being belongs to the "things" that populate the world with their solid and durable presence. But there are also other modes—like imaginary beings and fictional beings—the varieties of which will have to be studied in due course. Generally speaking, we can say that the modes of existence are all ways of occupying space-time, but only if we clarify that each mode creates the space-time it occupies. The space-time of phenomena is not the same as the space-time of things, and the space-time of things is not the same as the space-time of imaginary beings, and so on.

And in *L'Instauration philosophique* Souriau constructs a vast cosmos in which the whole array of different philosophies coexist with one another. The history of philosophy as a star chart or planetarium, the unfolding of a constellation of worlds, which thought's explorations cause to grow farther and farther apart. All these worlds compose a strange Monadology of divergent perspectives.[17] "We must initially admit the plurality of philosophemes, which is to say, the multiplicity of and real difference between the various attempts made by the human mind to inform the world philosophically. We must observe that the cosmos virtually contains a great number of equivalent solutions to the problem of its being informed" (IP, 214). The history of philosophy isn't unified by a destiny, or by progress; instead, it presents itself as a "pleroma," which is to say, as a world whose plenitude is ceaselessly enriched with new entities through the creation of new systems in as many distinct philosophical "gestures."[18] There is nothing peaceful or indifferent about this coexistence, however, since, as we know, a philosopher doesn't introduce new entities without at the same time criticizing the well-founded entities belonging to other systems.

What use are these classifications? What's Souriau after with these varied philosophical inventories? We said before that he wants to explore the variety of modes of existence included between being and nothingness, to traverse the gradation of existences from the fleeting radiance of the phenomenon up to the uncertain existence of virtual realities. There are entire populations of beings that escape the classic alternatives, "special presences" situated between being and nothingness, between the subjective and the objective, between the possible and the real, the self and the nonself.[19] "Will knowledge have to sacrifice entire populations of beings to Truth, stripping them of all their existential positivity; or, in order to admit them, will it have to divide the world into two, into three?" (DME, 103). One gets the impression that these are the populations that Souriau is particularly interested in. Everything takes place as if he wanted for his inventories to prevent the destruction of the variety of forms of existence that populate the world—and among them, especially, of the most fragile, the most evanescent, and also the most spiritual forms.

Souriau wants to serve as an advocate for these modes of existence. And the persona[20] of the advocate does not simply come to mind by chance: it haunts his books like one of the "conceptual personae" defined by Deleuze and Guattari. When they create this concept, Deleuze and Guattari make use of relational, dynamic, and existential features, but above all else they make use of juridical features.[21] How many portraits are there of philosophers as investigators, legislators, and judges, always depicted with court in full session? One might expect that, in Souriau, the juridical features would be downplayed in favor of "aesthetic" or existential features, but more often than not the opposite is the case. Behind the aesthetic figures we see the profiles of personae belonging to the juridical sphere emerge.

Thus, for example, behind the perceiving subject, we see the figure of the *witness* take shape. This is because, for Souriau, aesthetic perception is never neutral or disinterested—on the contrary. Certain privileged perceptions provoke our desire to testify "in favor" of the importance or the beauty of what we saw. In such a case, perceiving is not simply apprehending the perceived but wanting to testify or attest to the value of the perceived. The witness is never neutral or impartial. The responsibility falls on the witness *to show* what she has had the privilege of seeing, feeling, or thinking. This is the person who becomes a creator. At first a perceiving subject (seeing), she becomes a creating subject (showing). But this is because, behind the witness, the profile of another persona emerges: that of the advocate. It is the advocate who calls the witness to the stand and who makes every act of creation into a plea in favor of the very existences it makes appear—and makes appear before the court. We need to lend strength and scope to those things we've had the privilege of witnessing. That's why the artists and philosophers—whatever their role might be, otherwise—are also advocates whose various systems make pleas in favor of the new entities they instaur and whose legitimacy they seek to establish. They make new entities exist and produce new realities where no one had ever seen or conceived anything before: Plato's Idea, Aristotle's substance, Descartes's cogito, Leibniz's monad, and so on. How could they fail to become advocates for these realities, when they need to overcome all the skepticism, objections, and scorn that accompany their instauration?

Ultimately, Souriau's philosophy may be just as much a legal philosophy or a philosophy of rights as it is a philosophy of art. Perhaps art is even entirely at the service of rights and legitimization. Making certain existences "more" real, providing them with a foundation or a particular radiance—is that not a way of legitimizing their manner of being, of conferring upon them the right to exist in one form or another? This implies that every new form of existence is preceded, as it were, by a question that subterraneously undermines its reality: *quid juris*. By what right do you claim to exist? What legitimates the way in which you "posit" existence? Each new philosophical entity, but also each artistic, scientific, or existential form of existence, must prove that it is well founded [*bien-fondé*]. To "posit" themselves, they must also overcome the doubt, skepticism, or denial that contests their right to exist.

If an existence needs to prove that it is well founded, doesn't that also mean that it depends upon a foundation, a *grounding*, that confers this legitimacy upon it? Art would then become the art of grounding (and the definition of philosophy would join back up with Plato's). Every existence, unjustified in itself, would receive its sense, truth, and reality from a superior grounding, just as a proxy [*fondé de pouvoir*] receives her power from a legal authority. Once grounded, the existence would "cast aside the loose earth and sand so as to come upon rock or clay."[22] The grounding doesn't just provide a foundation or a framework but confers legitimacy upon the modes of existence that it grounds. A strange transformation through which an existence acquires a new reality from the mere fact of being legitimized: it now exists fully and walks on firm ground.

But what happens when this grounding loses its authority and legitimacy? Or when its authority crushes certain existences and strips them of their reality? Do those existences then need to reclaim the reality they lack for themselves? That's the whole problem. How can an existence ensure *its own* legitimacy, all by itself? Maybe we find ourselves back in Kafka's situation, when he "needed to be provided at every instant with a new confirmation of [his] existence."[23] Where is this confirmation going to come from if one is denied even the right to exist? What does a being have left when even its mode of existence has been contested? What space-time can it still legitimately occupy? "I must just take my walks and that must be sufficient, but in compensation there is no place in all the world where I could not take my walks."[24] There's no longer any earth, no longer any ground on which to place one's feet.

Where can we find the means of legitimizing some singular mode of existence within that mode of existence itself? How can we make existences more real? Perhaps existences need to pass first through other existences to posit or consolidate themselves—and others through them, in turn. We don't exist by ourselves; we only really exist in making something else exist. Every existence needs *intensifiers* if it is going to heighten its reality. A being can only achieve its right to exist with the help of another—and, in doing so, it makes that other exist. Is that the true role of the advocate—to intensify the reality of existences? To fight on behalf of new rights? It's a question of rights, but rights and legitimization are themselves, now more than ever, a question of art: which instaurative "gestures" enable existences to legitimately "posit" themselves?

2

Modes of Existence

What exactly is the existential pluralism with which Souriau begins? It is initially presented in the form of an ontological atomism. Every being is a manner of being, and vice versa: every manner of being is a distinct being, existing in its own manner. "What is, is; and fully occupies its pure existence" (DME, 127). A pure existence is a mode of existence grasped in itself, without reference to any other. *Patefit.*[1] From this perspective, each existence is as perfect as it can be. A sunset, the facade of a building, an optical illusion, a dance of electrons, an isosceles triangle, an abstract idea. On this plane, there is no hierarchy, no possible evaluation. Existence does not admit of degrees; each existence possesses its own intrinsic and incomparable mode of being. This atomism is meant to contest the great ontological forms—whether monist, dualist, or analogical—the grand theological visions that arrange beings into tiered planes in relation to a supreme reality or a superior archetype. No ontological gradation is possible. We can no longer say that one existence is more real, more authentic, or more essential than another (than, for instance, an existence that lives inauthentically, subjected to the dominion of appearances or opinions . . .). Every existence is as real, as existent, and as authentic as all the others.

We can no longer evaluate modes of existence on the basis of their power of existing. There is no greater or lesser power of existing. On this plane, one being isn't more accomplished than another, even when compared with itself. To take one of Souriau's own examples, the "thin, slightly rosy vapor stand[ing] out upon the bluish evening sky" does not have less existence than "the solid and illuminated fulness of a superb and perfect cloud, the glory of a lovely evening" (DME, 125–27). From one moment to the next, the cloud grew, perhaps it gained in perfection, but it would be absurd to say that it gained in existence. Existence doesn't admit of more and less; it is a neutral concept in that regard. If a being alters the conditions of its reality, this "will not make it exist more" (DME, 127). But then, what does Souriau mean when he speaks of the accomplishment of beings, of their progress toward a greater perfection? Is it not a question of introducing intensive gradations into the heart of existence itself, of making what exists pass from a lesser to a greater perfection?

Phenomena

In reality, such processes are situated on a different level, one that departs from the strictly atomistic plane of modes to join back up with the plane on which modes combine with one another and pass back and forth between one another to form new, plurimodal entities. For the time being, however, we'll have to disregard this latter plane and continue to consider the modes in isolation. For example, how do we grasp the phenomenon's mode of existence, independently of the consciousness that perceives it? How do we think it in and for itself, in its own existence? In a certain way, the method Souriau follows is the opposite of the phenomenological reduction, which relates phenomena to the consciousness or to the *ego* to which they appear. To establish such a correlation is to have already made the phenomenon depend upon another mode of existence and shifted the perspective. The same difficulty occurs if we relate it to an essence, a substance, or a noumenon: we deform its proper mode of existence by making it depend upon another, which is supposedly more consistent or more real.[2]

Yet the phenomenon has a manner all its own of positing itself in its own perfection, a manner that distinguishes it from every other mode of existence. It unfolds itself in an instantaneous architectonic that gives it its unique tonality, its singular radiance. Souriau often makes use of the same examples. They are like moments of grace in nature, described in their sudden splendor: a pink cloud in the sky, a tree branch stirring in the wind, a mountain's crest illuminated by the setting sun—pure snapshots, snapped in and for themselves. The entire landscape is recast thanks to a single nuance. The phenomenon is this nuance itself. Or rather, the nuance is the "soul" of the phenomenon in the sense that it testifies to the action of a fleeting formal principle, which is independent of the sensible content or the matter of the phenomenon (DME, 135). It is through this sudden architectonic that the phenomenon claims its proper mode of existence, even if it dissipates immediately. In other words, there is an "art, immanent to the phenomenon" (DME, 138). The brief appearance and subsequent dissipation of a structure. The phenomenon therefore has nothing to do with sensation. Sensations are rather "the din of the phenomenon" (DME, 137) and usually just confuse and conceal the formal principle that gives the appearance of the phenomenon its structure. "The sensible content of the ensemble can be bracketed: it is its architectonic—a pure formal principle—that we can single out and regard as the soul and the key of that indubitable patuity" (DME, 135).

Things

Things, too, have a way all their own of positing themselves in existence, one which is completely distinct from that of phenomena. What is a thing? What must a thing do to exist as a thing? Like the phenomenon, it reveals itself, but, unlike the former, it persists across its various manifestations (DME, 140). As Bruno Latour and Isabelle Stengers write in their introduction to the new edition of *The Different Modes of Existence,* the thing is "what *maintains itself* through its manifestations—by contrast with the phenomenon, which was *nothing but* its manifestations (all of them)" (DME, 49). A thing conquers and possesses itself in a permanence across space-time. "That is the basis of its existence. As an art of existing, it is the conquest and realization, the effective possession of this presence that is

indifferent to its situation" (DME, 143). We are no longer carried away by the changing variety of phenomena; we are now
installed in a world of permanences.

And yet, perhaps we shouldn't even speak of *the* thing,
since, in Souriau, this concept always refers to distinct entities
or "*réités*." Here, again, we'll have to introduce distinctions or
specify that there is a great variety of things, each with its own
manner of maintaining itself through its space-time. The equilateral triangle is a thing, but a Schubert sonata is also a thing.
The Egyptian pyramids, Socrates, and an atom are all things,
even though they don't persist through space-time in the same
manner. Souriau offers an image to illustrate the differences
between such distinct "things." Imagine a sheet of paper, first
folded up into an accordion, then crumpled into a ball—and
then imagine that, in each case, a needle has been stuck through
it. There's only one needle and one single hole. But when we
unfold the paper, several holes appear, arranged differently according to the case: regularly, when the sheet was folded, ran-
domly, when it was crumpled. The thing, like the needle, is one,
but the manifestations of its permanence in space-time can be
as varied as the arrangement of the holes on the sheet. Thus,
for example, the equilateral triangle or any other "rational entity" can exist in such a manner that it is dispersed in several
places at the same time. "The equilateral triangle in itself is the
singular essence of diverse phenomenal appearances" (DME,
144)—as is also the case with a sonata, which can be performed
simultaneously in several different places or can be nowhere
at all for a certain period of time. Whatever the phenomenal
variations of these manifestations may be, they refer to a thing
that is numerically one and "indifferent" to concrete situations.

But unlike essences and rational or musical entities, other
things exist that are subject to the obligation of existing here
and now, namely, singular things. Socrates, the individual, can
have neither the ubiquity of the equilateral triangle nor the
outward intermittence of a sonata. He is confined to a form of
permanent presence that won't permit him any ubiquity whatsoever. "It is a shame that we can never be in two places at once.
But to always be in just one place, how much more stringent a
demand is that!" (DME, 144). This constraint, peculiar to singu-

lar things, is at the same time a definition of the body. The body
is not initially defined by its organic or physical characteristics
but by the permanent obligations to which it subjects the psyche. The body is, in the first place, a constraint. From this point
of view, because our own body persists and thrusts us into the
world, it is, for us, the first of all "things." "It is the first work,
the infantile masterpiece of the stage at which we have ceased
being simply phenomena" (DME, 150). With the body, we enter
into the world of things.

But this permanence is only an initial characteristic. For an
existence to be a thing, it needs to be bound up with others, it
must form a systematic unity with them and compose a history
that joins them together in a definite cosmos. The architectonic
of the phenomenon is transformed and becomes "cosmicity."
Socrates is inseparable from the whole context that makes him
what he is: Athens, its laws, its mores, the Greek language, and
so on. Likewise, the equilateral triangle is inseparable from a set
of axioms and the properties of Euclidian space, and the sonata
is bound to the rules of harmony, to the instruments needed for
performing it, and so on. There is, in the world of things, a "cosmicity," an organization, various systems of connections guaranteeing their stability—as opposed to the mercurial world of
phenomena and their evanescent architectonics. And yet, paradoxically, the permanence of things is not inherent in them; it
comes to them from psyches.

While the phenomenon owes its manner of existing only to
itself, the thing really owes its status as a thing to the psyche
that thinks it and, in doing so, posits its unity, its identity, and
its cosmicity. A thought is needed to keep the thing in existence,
beyond its phenomenal manifestations, and to constitute a
cosmos populated by interconnected things. But the thought,
here, is really nothing other than the relation by which the thing
is maintained in existence and connected with other things.[3]
Conversely, this means that "thought has no other support than
the very thing that it assembles and feels" (DME, 147). In other
words, thought is conditioned by the thing it maintains in existence, which, in return, gives thought its foundation.[4]

That's why *the mode of existence of thought is ultimately of
the same kind as the mode of existence of things*. If things form a

stable and systematic system, psyches also have a sort of "monumentality that makes of their organization and form the law of a permanence."[5] This doesn't mean that souls or psyches are things but that things are things through the soul that thinks them, just as the soul gains monumentality through its thinking of things, through its construction of an ordered world of various things, psyches, rational entities, and physical or practical entities. Psyches are not things, but they have the *structure* of a thing in the sense that they form "harmonic system[s] susceptible to modifications, enlargements, occasional corruptions, and even wounds . . ." (DME, 148). Here we are, then, in the presence of a second world. This is no longer the world of phenomena but *the cosmos of things*—a world in which psychic entities, rational entities, physical entities, and practical entities coexist as so many "*réités.*"[6] We can see that the criteria by which we distinguish between modes of existence are, before all else, structural and relative to the conditions in which a reality posits itself in its own mode of existence. These conditions describe the manner in which each mode of existence distributes itself in and occupies a definite space-time.

Imaginaries

To these modes of existence, we must still add all those "fragile and inconsistent entities," which double the world of things and thoughts—or of psyches and *réismes*, to speak like Souriau. They are so fragile, he explains, that we might be hesitant even to grant them an existence. They are the fictional beings, all those imaginary beings that "exist for us with an existence based in desire, concern, fear, or hope, or even fancy and diversion" (DME, 153). They obey neither the phenomenon's logic of appearance nor the thing's law of identity, though they do imitate the status of such modes in the sense that an imagined dog does relate to an existing dog. This is the case with all fictional characters. To be sure, they can't be inserted into the cosmos of things, they can't become things among other things, since they don't obey any logic of appearance or any law of identity. In this sense, they suffer from "acosmicity." Nevertheless, they do belong to microcosms, which form quasi-worlds.

These beings have what we might call a social existence, in that they belong to the discourses, references, and beliefs of a given cultural world. Then why not grant them the same status as things? Don't Don Quixote and Swann have a foundation at least as assured as that of psyches? In reality, fictional beings don't derive their means of subsistence from social interaction, even if they are a part of it. What makes them exist is our beliefs. If Don Quixote or Swann exists, it is by virtue of our "solicitude," says Souriau; that's what makes them exist in the first place. If Souriau defines them as "solicitudinary" beings, rather than as imaginaries, it is because their existence depends upon the affects that participate in their instauration.[7] How many beings owe their existence to fear or desire? How many monsters fill the darkness for a child at night?

To say that these beings exist isn't to say that they have a merely "subjective" existence but that they make us act, speak, and think in relation to the manner of being our beliefs impart upon them. These are the monsters of the night that make the child take to her heels. What distinguishes them from the *réique* existence of things is that they cease to exist as soon as they are no longer supported by these affects or beliefs. Their mode of existence is no longer substantial but, insofar as it feeds upon our affects, "sustentive."[8] They lack the ubiquity, the cosmic insertion, or the consistency necessary to be things (DME, 154). To the world of phenomena and the cosmos of things, we must therefore add *the kingdom of fictions,* which includes all imaginary beings—or rather the ensemble of possible beings, which, for Souriau, is always a species of the imaginary (DME, 150–56). Beings that are imagined, dreamed, deemed possible, fantasized—a whole host of beings, some momentary, some almost as solid as things.[9]

Virtuals

But there are beings of an even lesser existence, if such a thing can even be said. Souriau describes a kind of existence still more tenuous, still more fragile, than the fictional beings, namely, *virtual beings.* "Is saying that a thing exists virtually, the same as saying that it does not exist? Not at all. But neither is it

saying that the thing is possible. It is saying that some reality
conditions it, without thereby including or positing it. Closed in
upon itself in the void of a pure nothingness, it completes itself
outwardly. The broken or newly begun arch of a bridge virtually
outlines the missing section" (DME, 156). These beings are beginnings, sketches, monuments that don't yet exist and maybe
never will. Maybe the bridge will never be restored, maybe the
draft will never be completed, the story never continued . . .
Unlike the solicitudinaries, the mode of existence of virtuals
doesn't depend on an affect, nor does it receive its reality from
the power of our beliefs. There must, however, be something
about them that prevents them from being confused with
pure nothingness: repairing the bridge, extending the curve,
developing something from the slightest indication, in short,
making these virtualities exist, can only happen according to
certain conditions, which are dictated, in part, by the existing
sketch *but also, in part, by the virtualities themselves*—and this
means that they cannot be confused with nonexistence, pure
and simple.

An example that illustrates the nature of these virtuals particularly well can be found in Henry James, when he describes
his method of composing a novel. Sometimes, during a dinner,
it happens that he hears a suggestive anecdote, "a mere float-
ing particle in the stream of talk," in which he glimpses what
might become the "subject" of a new story. "One's subject is in
the merest grain, the speck of truth, of beauty, of reality, scarce
visible to the common eye." Thus, when he hears tell of a dis-
pute between a mother and her son concerning the furniture
of an old house, he senses that it has the basic framework of a
new story (this will become the novella *The Spoils of Poynton*).
"There had been but ten words, yet I had recognized in them, as
in a flash, all the possibilities of the little drama of my 'Spoils,'
which glimmered then and there into life; so that when in the
next breath I began to hear of action taken . . . I saw clumsy
Life again at her stupid work."[10] This is a beautiful description
of the way the virtual reveals itself: the appearance of a range
of new possibilities, dictated by several barely sketched traits.
Yet the ordinary course of life does not succeed in maintaining the lofty, architectonic promises that the virtual allows us to

behold. Life "persistently blunders and deviates, loses herself in the sand." Unless the opposite is the case: rather than follow the ordinary course of the conversation, the writer splits off in the direction of a parallel universe, the possibilities of which his story will explore.

Up to now, we have distinguished three universes: the world of phenomena, the cosmos of things, and the kingdom of fictions. We must now add to them a fourth: *the ephemeral swarm of virtuals.* "A number of sketches or starts, a number of interrupted indications outline, around an inferior and changing reality, a whole kaleidoscopic interplay of beings or monumentalities that will never exist" (DME, 156). The virtuals are there, all around us; they appear, disappear, and transform along with the changes of reality itself; they have no solidity, no foundation, no consistency. In certain respects, at least in appearance, this universe is the richest and most vast—but it is also the most evanescent, the least consistent, and the closest to nothingness.

In the—nonexhaustive—inventory of modes of existence that Souriau draws up,[11] the virtuals seem to have a special status. Every mode of existence bears witness to a specific "art"—an art of appearing for phenomena, an art of persisting for things, an art of sustaining (or of being sustained) for imaginaries—and virtuals are not exempt from this rule. An "art" presides over the perfection of their manner of being. Only, their perfection is the perfection of being incomplete; they are perfectly, intrinsically incomplete. Which is to say, there is in them something like an expectation of or a demand for accomplishment.

That is what sets them apart. They await the art that can make them exist more and otherwise. Theirs is the art of provoking or demanding art; their proper "gesture" is the provocation of other gestures. They need another being—a creator—to do everything in its power to make them exist more and in a different mode. Conversely, the creator needs this volatile cloud of virtuals to create new realities; it is nourished by their incompletion. In other words, *it is the virtuals themselves that introduce a desire for creation and a will to art into the world.*

They are the source of all the arts we practice. The arts, philosophy, the sciences—they never cease nourishing themselves on
this unremitting and ephemeral swarm of "specks of truth" that
lines our world.

This isn't to say that they constitute a different universe, a
universe separate from the real world. On the contrary, they are
completely immanent to this world. Snippets of conversation
become the germ of a story, a face's features are transformed
into a potential portrait, several notes form the beginning of a
melody, a screenplay becomes a film, an intuition becomes a
system, and so on. There is no reality that isn't accompanied by
an evanescent host of potentialities, following it like its shadow.
Each existence can become a motive, a suggestion, or the germ
of something else, a fragment of a new, future reality. Every existence becomes incomplete by right. In other words, a second
panel of Souriau's philosophy opens up with the virtuals. The
initial atomism, which permitted us to draw up the inventory
of the modes of existence as elements or "semantemes" of a
modal ontology, is abandoned (DME, 169). Now existences can
be modified, transformed; they can intensify their reality, pass
from one mode to another, or combine modes. We enter the
realm of the *transmodal*. If the virtuals hold a privileged place
in Souriau, it is because they are the main engine driving the
passage from the modal to the transmodal. We pass from a
static world, in which the modes of existence are described for
themselves, to a dynamic world, in which it is the transformations, the augmentations and diminutions, that will henceforth
matter.

This isn't to say that when the virtuals pass into existence,
they cease to exist as virtuals—on the contrary. It is the virtuals themselves that dictate the conditions of their passage
into existence, despite their indistinction. Each creative effort, each step forward, is like a proposed existence, to which
the virtual either does or does not consent, depending on the
ever-changing demands of its still-nascent architectonic. Proposed words, colors, lines and spaces, compositions, forms—in
each case, a possibility is implicitly submitted to the virtual,
turned toward it so as to learn whether it accepts the option
in question. Each virtual has a manner all its own of accepting

or, should they express it inadequately, rejecting such propositions; it takes shape as much through the affirmations as through the successive negations with which it surrounds itself and which make it into a problematic being.[12] Moreover, every instauration of a new reality must either disperse the phantoms and take their place or be toppled by them.[13]

Without a doubt, these terms are inappropriate. In reality, virtuals don't dictate; they neither accept nor reject anything. Rather, they form a nebula in which every decision becomes a matter of presentiment, divination, or intuition. Moreover, most of the conditions that these virtuals "dictate" arc as implicit as they are changeable. But that doesn't prevent them from acting as imperiously as any other kind of reality. They have the force of a *problem*. The virtuals have a *problematizing force*, of which Henry James offers a very precise formulation: "If life, presenting us the germ . . . gives the case away, almost always, before we can stop her, what are the signs for our guidance, what the primary laws for a saving selection, how do we know when and where to intervene, where do we place the beginnings of the wrong or the right deviation?"[14]

Such is the question Souriau never stops posing. Such is the general question of experimentation or of what he calls *instauration*. Again, if the virtuals have such importance for him, it is because they make us enter a new dimension: no longer that of the modes of existence (the modal) but that of their transformations into and out of one another (the transmodal). How can a being at the limit of nonexistence attain a more "real," more consistent existence? With what gesture? What is the "art" that allows existences to heighten their reality?[15] It is certainly the most fragile existences, nearly nothing, that forcefully insist upon becoming more real. Still, we must be capable of perceiving them, of grasping their value and importance. So much so that, before we can pose the question of the creative act that allows us to instaur them, we need to ask what it is that allows us to perceive them in the first place.

3

How to See

With what one word convey its change? Careful. Less. Ah the sweet one word. Less. It is less. The same but less. Whencesoever the glare.

—Samuel Beckett

I am thinking of a little child who had very carefully and at great length arranged a variety of objects of differing sizes upon his mother's table, making sure that their array be decorative and pleasing, in order to give her a "great delight." The mother arrives. Relaxed, distracted, she grabs one of the objects, something she needs, moves another back to its usual place, undoes it all. And when the child's barely stifled sobs give way to desperate explanations, revealing to her the extent of her error, she cries out, full of regret, "Oh! My poor little angel, I hadn't seen that there was something there!"

—Étienne Souriau, *Avoir une âme*

I hadn't seen. . . . But what is it that she doesn't see? What is the "something" that the mother fails to see? We might say that it is the careful arrangement of the objects, testament to the child's particular point of view. Or we might say that it is the child's "soul," transferred entirely over into the arrangement. Either way, we would be right: she certainly sees the objects, since she tidies them up—what she doesn't see is the mode of existence that belongs to them from the child's point of view, the architectonic that they sketch out in the child's eyes. *What she doesn't see is the child's point of view*; she doesn't see that *there is* a point of view, a point of view that exists in a manner all its own. It is a virtuality that she fails to perceive, just as a distracted hiker fails to see the sketch of a virtual bridge in the rows of stones lined up across from one another on opposite banks of a stream. They are like spectators standing before an anamorphosis, who, failing to find the angle that would allow them to decipher it, can't see what it represents. There are openings in the cosmos of things, innumerable openings marked out by virtuals. Rare are those who perceive these openings and attribute any importance to them; rarer still are those who delve into them with creative experimentation.

This blindness doesn't apply only to virtuals but already appears at the level of phenomena, when, having so often taken them to be manifestations of a persisting thing, we miss their pure phenomenality. We take the phenomenality from the phenomenon and attribute it to that of which the phenomenon is supposed to be a manifestation. "Initially manifest, the phenomenon thus becomes manifestation; initially appearance, it becomes apparition" (DME, 133). Trees are in bloom before me, radiant against the backdrop of tall grasses and a clear sky— that's what appears. But the phenomenon is neither the tree, nor the grass, nor the sky; it is something else entirely: "There is a freshness and an authority to the hues; the colors press in upon one another, both in opposition and in harmony; the rosy white radiance of the sun; the poignant picture of a single, little bouquet of flowers at the end of a branch upon the turquoise blue of the sky"—*that* is the phenomenality of the phenomenon, a sort of architectonic to which even the slightest thing could lay waste: the soul of the moment. We have seen that Souriau takes care always to distinguish the formal principle of the phenomenon from its content. This principle is the armature of the phenomenon, the manner in which it makes the various elements composing it "hold" together according to harmonic relations of opposition, contrast, complementarity, or equilibrium.

The story of the mother and child is like an echo of the famous Brancusi controversy. Let us briefly recall the scene. In October 1926, as twenty or so sculptures were being unloaded onto American soil, the *Bird in Space* caught the attention of a New York Harbor customs inspector, who, after examining it, refused to grant the long piece of bronze the exemption works of art legally receive. Instead, he imposed on it the tax usually applied to manufactured commercial objects. This customs inspector is like the mother from Souriau's example: he doesn't see anything but a simple piece of bronze. He doesn't see the "soul" or the point of view enveloped in the form, the architectonic it unfolds, in short, the mode of existence that belongs to it from a certain point of view. We can see how quickly the problem becomes a legal problem of *rights*: not just because the controversy, brought before the courts, enabled the transformation of the legal status of works of art in the United States but also because, for Brancusi, it was a matter of doing justice to new forms of life.[1]

Why is it that the composition of the phenomenon isn't any easier to perceive than was the child's careful arrangement of objects on a table? For one simple reason: because we perceive it from the perspective of a point of view that relies upon a different kind of data for the continuity of its world to be established and guaranteed. We have to clear off the table, apply the customs regulations, and so on. Do we not, then, need to break with the natural attitude, so as to gain access to a renewed consciousness of the phenomenon and thereby return "to the things themselves," as phenomenology hopes to do? But, in Souriau's eyes, phenomenology doesn't come any closer to grasping the "soul" of the phenomenon, despite its methodological precautions. It grasps things, not from the inside, but from the outside, according to the point of view of the observing consciousness. Its perspective is always that of consciousness, never that of the phenomenon itself. "The phenomenological dialectic brackets the phenomenon itself in its real presence and immediacy, explicating and accomplishing it separately, from without, in order to preserve and to look only—which is what the phenomenon implies and requires by moving toward something other than itself. So much so that, in this sense, phenomenology is the place where we are least likely to find the phenomenon. As Kim says, *The darkest place is under the lamp*" (DME, 136).[2] Like the mother with her child, phenomenology doesn't see that there is a point of view *internal* to the phenomenon itself.

But what exactly does it mean to grasp something from the inside? How are we to understand the idea that the phenomenon expresses a point of view? That it is animated by a perspective all its own? Perceiving, for Souriau, is not observing, from the outside, a world spread out before you; on the contrary, it is *entering* into a point of view, as when we sympathize. Perception is participation. A phenomenon takes place, its beauty strikes us, and there we are, seized inside a sort of perceptual monument, exploring its momentary composition from within. Our perspective is inserted into another perspective— our point of view is inserted into another point of view—as if there were an intentionality or, better, an organizing principle visible within the architectonic of the phenomenon itself. We don't have a perspective on the world; it is actually the world that makes us enter into one of its perspectives. Being isn't closed in upon itself, withdrawn into an inaccessible in-itself, but is opened up endlessly by the perspectives it provokes. Perspectives open Being up, unfold it, explore its dimensions and planes, which are by right innumerable.

But how are we to do this? How are we to show these perspectives? Would it be possible for us to devise a method for showing these compositions, once we have established that to show something is to make it exist, to make it more real by rendering it perceptible? We know that there must be an "art" for this. We would have to devise a sort of optical apparatus that would allow us to perceive these perspectives and give them a more manifest reality. One such method is the *reduction*. Indeed, to make the variety of modes of existence appear, Souriau appeals to something like an "existential" reduction—though it isn't clear that this adjective is quite right. To be sure, the reduction he carries out is meant to be the exact antithesis of the phenomenological reduction, in that, in each individual instance, it is a question of extracting the point of view expressed by some mode of existence or other, rather than of subordinating them all to the point of view of consciousness.[3] Each mode of existence possesses a singular "plane of existence," which is the basis of its unfolding. But the operation is less "existential" than perspectivist, since describing a mode of existence entails *returning, in each instance, to the interior of the point of view it expresses.* Each mode of existence envelops a point of view; in fact, that is what distinguishes it from existence, pure and simple. Souriau often repeats: we need to find the thing's point of view, for each mode of existence possesses its own point of view.

What, then, does he mean by "reduction" here? Husserl reinvents the term, but not the operation, which is as old as philosophy itself. In general, the importance of the reduction is the instauration of a plane that makes the perception of new entities possible. The reduction becomes a method, but it is well known that this method's primary function is to act upon perception, to bring about a conversion of the gaze. It is a matter of *showing,* of rendering new classes of otherwise invisible beings perceptible.[4] Hence a first moment, which consists in ridding the plane of all the presuppositions, prejudices, and illusions that stand in the way of this renewal of perception. The reduction is, in the first place, an act of cleansing. The field must be purified of everything that stands in the way of seeing.

In this sense, to reduce is to extract a plane of pure existence. But purified of what? What must be removed before we can finally see? The responses clearly vary from one philosopher to the next. Plato, the first, describes characters who bring about the conversion that is necessary for seeing what the others, prisoners of appearances, cannot: the world of essences. What needs to be eliminated is the changing reality of sensible appearances, which inhibits our contemplation of the world of Ideas. This world constitutes a plane of pure experience where "pure" designates the Idea's form of self-identity: the Just in itself, the Beautiful in itself, the Good in itself. The Ideas are pure forms in the sense that they are free of all alterity, of all alteration. And only a thought that has become pure thought *(noûs)* can contemplate them. Then, in Descartes, there is the intervention of doubt, which allows us to purify the field of experience of all that is external to the pure interiority of the "I think." We no longer seek a form of identity that would be free of all alterity, as in Plato, but a form of interiority that would be free of any external element craftily seeking its way in. And the same is the case with the phenomenological reduction, which, once it has rid itself of all naturalist presuppositions, seeks to establish transcendental egology as "purely inner psychology."[5] There, too, it's a matter of mapping out a plane designed to show what would otherwise remain invisible: the originary world of the essences of our lived experience. Plato, Descartes, Husserl: three kinds of reduction for three modes of the perception of essences.

But not every reduction aims to show essences or substances. Some even pursue a goal that is completely opposed to such an aim. While it is always a matter of constituting a plane of pure experience, some rid the plane of any and every form of preexisting identity or interiority. Experience is pure if it has been purified of every last trace of essence or consciousness—instead of being reduced to a "pure consciousness."[6] No more essence, no more form of interiority, we begin from the degree zero of experience to *show* how lived experiences are constituted. Neither the presuppositions we fight against nor the personae we encounter are the same as in the previous cases. We are no longer dealing with personae who are prisoners of a false knowledge but with ignorant personae who are deprived entirely of understanding, such as the figures of the newborn or Adam.[7] Or even Condillac's strange statue, which embodies the degree zero of sensitivity. The philosophers of the seventeenth and eighteenth centuries uncover a new plane of observation on which the reduction becomes the product of an analysis: what do we perceive when experience is decomposed into its most simple elements? "Pure" is no longer the essential or the substantial but the elementary or the simple. It is on the basis of this new plane that we see the complex experiences of intellectual, moral, and political subjects constituted. It is the same operation as when, in political philosophy, the degree zero converges with a "state of nature," which is conceived as an experience purified of all political organization. The state of nature acts as an apparatus on the basis of which we can finally *see* the formation of political bodies.

If the reduction is inseparable from the planes of pure experience it instaurs, we can see that it also needs personae to reveal these planes. Plato needs a prisoner to exit the cave. Deleuze and Guattari have shown that it was absolutely necessary for philosophies to introduce personae, in order for them to equip themselves with a pair of eyes, populate the plane they trace, and animate their concepts. Souriau would have certainly appreciated this hypothesis, which strengthens the thesis of an art immanent to philosophy.[8] From one type of reduction to the other, the personae are not at all the same. In the case of the reduction we might broadly label "rationalist," we meet with doubters, wary of appearances, or false skeptics in search of the truth, as in Plato, Descartes, and Husserl. In the other case—which we might call "empiricist"—we meet with the ingenuous, the naive, and the ignorant. This is the case with figures such as Adam or the newborn in classical empiricism but also with the naïf in William James's radical empiricism; with the man of "common sense" in Bergson's metaphysical empiricism at the beginning of *Matter and Memory,* ignorant of all philosophical disputes;[9] and even with Deleuze and Guattari's Spinozist *homo natura* in *Anti-Oedipus,* which is linked to the Nietzschean child at play in *What Is Philosophy?* The personae of empiricist philosophies no longer aim for essences. They have a certain innocence in common, which is why they are without presuppositions and are *open to all the potentialities of pure experience.* Their opennesss to the greatest heterogeneity possible is, paradoxically, their manner of being "pure." They are profoundly "impure," in this sense: they are capable of all sorts of metamorphoses, of maintaining several perspectives at once, and of shifting back and forth between them. The empiricist persona is therefore no longer engaged in an effort to reach the substantial or essential for the simple reason that, on this new plane, there is no more "self," and there are no more substances or essences.

One might object that such apparatus are worthless outside of philosophy—that in the arts, for instance, no such reduction

takes place. And yet, don't we also encounter in the arts attempts to establish a plane that will allow us to see what would
otherwise remain invisible, and to get back to a sort of pure experience, on the basis of which we can then begin to rebuild? In
literature, we see this in the existence of characters who seem
to result from a process of reduction, insofar as they embody
a form of pure experience. They get back to a kind of degree
zero. These characters don't know more than others. On the
contrary, they have retained an innocence, a naivety of which
others are no longer capable; their very nature seems to guard
them against any shameful compromises and makes them into
privileged observers. Diderot's *Nun*; Dostoevsky's *Idiot*; the
religious, younger *Karamazov* brother; the children or young
Americans in Henry James; the child in *Germany Year Zero*;
and the haunted young soldier in Klimov's masterpiece, *Come
and See*, among so many others—they embody the process
of reduction in the way they make us see differently. And not
only do they make us see the baseness, maliciousness, and dis-
honor of those around them but they also make us see the fact
that others don't even notice, that they've long since stopped
seeing. These characters act as mirrors or "intensifiers" of
experience.[10]

The visual arts are engaged in the same struggle when they
come up against the necessity of making the page, canvas, or
screen entirely black or entirely white so as to start all over
again—a pure experience or degree zero meant to cleanse our
perception. How can we fail to see Rauschenberg's series of
White Paintings, then his *Black Paintings*—or the "grids" from
which Agnes Martin repeatedly starts off—as a reduction of
painting to a form of pure experience?[11] It is no longer a question of bringing painting to its ultimate limit or supposed essence: absolute White or Black as painting's quintessence. It
isn't a question of isolating a form or a pure quality, any more
than it is a question of reaching a pure matter. Instead, it is a
question of starting from a sort of part physical, part mental
material that recharges the potentials of painting. For what distinguishes a material from mere matter is that it is animated
by forces, by internal dynamisms that make it a quasi-mental,
living reality. Wood and stone are not inert matter but are shot

through with folds, veins, and knots that give them their movement. Material is matter becoming mind.[12]

Every effort really consists in raising yourself to the level of your material and of following its vectors, its "intentionalities"—and therefore in renouncing the intentionality of consciousness, even if it is the source of sense. As Dubuffet (who also calls for a man of common sense) says, "the mind is set in motion by what is presented to it; it adheres to it completely and falls into line with it. . . . Art should emerge from the material and the tool, it should retain the trace of the tool and its struggle with the material."[13] Follow the potentialities of the material, even and especially when they lead to unexpected connections, so as to become its closest collaborator. "Pure" no longer refers to essences but to a composite material capable of transformations and metamorphoses—a little like those mollusks that protect themselves by adorning themselves with fragments of shells, coral branches, and stones, which they utilize as if they were parts of their own bodies, or, better yet, like one of Rauschenberg's paintings, in which he mixes pigments, pieces of mirror, socks, newspaper clippings, a fan, glue, metal, a bunch of truly "impure" elements (cf. *Rebus, Charlene, Broadcast,* or *Pantomime*). Such works are only possible if all presuppositions regarding essence have been shed. The work is then made by connection, through the multiple links between "inessential" elements that are brought together at one point or another.

And art's personae are also transformed. There are no longer just unified—saintly or Christ-like—figures but also composite figures that are patched up or cobbled together. A good example from literature is the evolution of the Robinson character. Having lost everything in the shipwreck, Robinson was the ideal character for embodying the degree zero of experience. Was that not the perfect occasion for him to shed all of his prejudices, for him to rid himself of all his presuppositions and illusions? And yet, instead, we see him take up the same tasks as ever: build, exploit, organize, capitalize—a colonizer down to his very soul. The situation barely changes with the best-known Robinsonades (like those by Johann David Wyss or Jules Verne). For it to become relevant again, both in literature and in philosophy, the shipwreck had to become a veritable process of reduction, from which Robinson would emerge profoundly changed and capable of seeing what no one else could see. That's precisely what Michel Tournier describes in *Friday; or, The Other Island*. Robinson becomes the figure of a pure experience: the experience of a world without others. The organization of his world disintegrates gradually as the presence of others fades. All his presuppositions, all his prejudices, all his illusions are swept away. A new world then appears, a primordial world in which Robinson is exposed to all sorts of metamorphoses. We know that Deleuze was interested in this novel because he, too, conceived of the reduction as a sort of desertification. To reduce, for Deleuze, is to desertify, which is to say, to explore the powers of matter and thought by placing them in a world before or after humanity.[14] Then, more recently and following a different trajectory, Robinson becomes a polymorphic, composite, and dispersed figure, as in the stories of Olivier Cadiot. There, Robinson becomes "zero sum," the experience of a cogito permanently reduced to zero by the entropic proliferation of changing states, ceaselessly scattering him into so many possible versions of himself.[15] Robinson is no longer the revelator of a world without others; he becomes a succession of unconnected sequences, the real and mental space in which all others crash into each other like the debris of a permanent shipwreck.

If we have referred to planes and personae as tools of the reduction, this is because Souriau himself makes profound use of these notions. His modal ontology is inseparable from a plurality of planes of existence with their varied personae. His book *Avoir une âme* is exemplary in this respect, because it is organized around brief sequences of fiction. Souriau multiplies the personae in order to make us enter into their perspectives: each is the illustration of an art of existing, and while some of these are illusory, others are fully accomplished. That is the significance of the perspectivist reduction that Souriau carries out: by right, we are only ever dealing with perspectives and with the planes of existence that each perspective traces for itself. It is still a matter of attaining a pure experience, but, in this case, what disappears is the preexistence of *a common, external world*. That is the next presupposition to be dismantled. This isn't to say that there is no longer a world or that its existence is put in parentheses as with the phenomenological epoché. Rather, the world becomes internal to the perspectives and is thereby multiplied.[16] What disappears, then, is not the world but the idea of a *common* world. The perspectivist thesis is that there is not, in the first place, a common world, which each being then appropriates and makes into "its own" world, but the inverse. First, there are singular, "private" worlds that then form a common world through their multiple communications. The world becomes common through the communication of "private" worlds instead of an initially common world becoming privatized into private worlds. Instead of a common world, a multiplicity of manners or gestures: manners of perceiving it, of appropriating it, or of exploring its potentialities. The error lies in believing that the perspectives are added from the outside to a preexisting world, "on" which they have a point of view. Once again, they are not external to the world; the world, on the contrary, is internal to the perspectives (AA, 24). Zero is the point of conversion. It is the birth of the perspective, while "less than zero" would be the mark of its dissolution in a world that is common, all too common.[17]

At this point, let us draw out a few essential features of Souriau's thought. We can see that it is presented as a *pluralist* ontology, because Being is grasped on the basis of its modes, which are so many arts of existence. It then appears as a *perspectivist* philosophy, because each mode is submitted to the "law of the point of view" that it expresses. And this perspectivism is inseparable from a *formalism*, because each point of view expresses, in its own manner, a structure or an architectonic, which constitutes the law of its potential development. Finally, these two aspects come together in a *spiritualism*, because the point of view (or the architectonic) constitutes the soul of each mode of existence.

It is a sign of this perspectivism that Souriau describes his process of reduction as a succession of *adjustments*, which is to say, as an ensemble of "active operations, aiming to explicate a being by apprehending it at its highest degree of perfection"

(AA, 24). This, in part, is the meaning behind the microtales of *Avoir une âme*. It is necessary to enter into a perspective and follow it all the way to its point of accomplishment, its maximal point of "lucid presence" (AA, 24; IP, 247). Each existence must be brought to its greatest state, thereby instauring the plane that belongs to it in its own right. A perspective is actually defined less by its manner of being than by its modes of appropriation, less by its *being* than by its *having*.[18] This is a new sign of the passage from the modal to the transmodal: it is no longer a matter of being this or that but of claiming new manners of being as so many dimensions of oneself.

4

Distentio animi

You have to have a soul, and to have it, you have to make it.

—Étienne Souriau

When Souriau introduces virtuals into the inventory of modes of existence, everything changes. We can no longer maintain the initial atomism, according to which each existence is perfect in itself and definitively complete in its order. With virtuals, all reality becomes incomplete. This isn't only the case for the broken arch of a bridge or for a sketch but is true of every reality, even of a reality that is so complete we would say that it is "finished." The great truth, says Souriau, is "the existential incompletion of every thing. Nothing, not even our own selves, is given to us other that in a sort of half-light, a penumbra in which only incompleteness can be made out, where nothing possesses either full presence or evident patuity, where there is neither total accomplishment, nor plenary existence."[1]

If everything becomes a sketch, this entails an unavoidable consequence: there are no longer any beings, there are only processes. In other words, from this point on, the only entities will be *acts*: the changes, transformations, and metamorphoses that affect beings and make them exist otherwise. "Let us evoke a universe of existence wherein the only beings would be these

sorts of dynamisms or transitions: deaths, sublimations, spiri-
tualizations, births and rebirths. . . . The only reality would be
the immense drama or the ceremony of such acts" (DME, 171).
In Souriau's terminology, we are no longer in the ontic world
but in the *synaptic* world, a world of transformations, events,
and occurrences. We pass from the modal to the transmodal. To
be sure, we can always return to the initial inventory and range
the event alongside the phenomenon, the thing, imaginary
entities, and so on—but on one condition: we have to admit
that existence is no longer only "in beings, but between them"
(DME, 106). It is nevertheless the case that this new mode of
existence makes us pass over into a different world, one with
"an entirely different existential poise."[2]

It is a world in which there are no longer things but only
verbs and conjugations of verbs. We might believe ourselves to
be in the book Borges imagined, which describes the world of
Tlön as no longer being "a concourse of objects in space" but a
"heterogenous series of independent acts." It is a world that is
purely "successive and temporal, not spatial," to such an extent
that "there are no nouns in Tlön's conjectural *Ursprache,* from
which the 'present' languages and the dialects are derived:
there are impersonal verbs, modified by monosyllabic suffixes
(or prefixes) with an adverbial value. For example, there is no
word corresponding to the word 'moon,' but there is a verb
which in English would be 'to moon' or 'to moonate.'"[3] When
the mother, in the brief tale from *Avoir une âme,* said, "It was
something," she placed herself in the ontic world. In the synaptic world, we must now say, "Something is happening."

What is the nature of what happens for Souriau? How does
he understand the event? Take a shattering glass, for instance.
"A moment ago, there was a whole glass; now there are these
pieces. Between the two, there is the irreparable. . . . *There is* the
'to shatter.' The having occurred, the fact of the fact[4]—that remains irreducible. One form alone truly expresses this: the verbality of the verb, of the part of speech in which the difference
between 'to come' and 'coming,' between 'to fall' and 'falling,'
'fell,' or 'will fall' is expressed. . . . The patuity of this irreducibil-
ity. Such is the existence of the fact" (DME, 173). Let's not allow
the example to mislead us. What is important here is the *reality*

of the fact, not the fact itself. The importance of the fact lies in the indubitable character of its reality. We can doubt the reality of certain existences but not of facts, for they have an effectiveness, they change something in the mode of existence of beings. The effectiveness, here, is not the fact that the glass is broken but the fact that its mode of being changes. It is no longer a glass but a bunch of jagged shards. In keeping with Souriau's perspectivism, the event consists in *a reversal of the point of view*: something has happened, which has made it such that we can no longer regard the glass as a glass. In this sense, the event is strictly *spiritual*. We are like the child who, having just broken a glass, points to each object in her vicinity and asks, "Breakable?" For the child, the world is no longer the same; from now on it will be grasped as something "breakable" and populated with things that break. One instant was enough . . . for everything to be perceived differently. Again, there is nothing material about the event ("the fact"); it is purely spiritual ("the fact of the fact"), or "incorporeal," as the Stoics would say—it is the life of the mind.

One instant was enough . . . In Souriau, the instant, understood as being "instaurative" or "prerogative," is clearly privileged. It is the same privilege he accords to virtuals. This is because, for Souriau, the instant is *the time of the virtual*. Certain instants—certain virtuals—constitute events in the sense that they determine a vocation or a destiny. *Patefit.* The instant is the time, or rather the meantime, of events. We should conceive of the course of time as a hallway, all along which instants would be lined like doors, each opening onto a different world; through each one, we glimpse a perfection, we sense that there is "more" reality, as Pessoa did on his walk. It is an existential summit, a lucid point penetrating through what exists, in Souriau's terms. Will it remain isolated, a pure atom with no continuance, or will it join with other moments to give their existence a new architectonic?

Once again, sometimes these instants play a decisive role, disrupting psyches and opening them up to different perspectives.[5] Souriau gives lovely examples of these reversals of points of view, such as the story of the phantom, born of a desire for revenge, who questions the meaning of his presence and returns

to nothingness when he discovers he no longer wishes to wreak
vengeance upon the woman he once loved:

> As soon as we seriously question ourselves about
> our being, each of us is, to one extent or another,
> this ghost. For, instead of feeling included and en-
> gaged in a world—a world which would usually
> answer for and support him, and which would pre-
> vent him from asking the question, "Am I?"—he,
> too, is led to ask this question for some reason. But
> why? Because, for a moment, he agreed to answer
> for the world, instead of leaving it to the world to
> answer for him. And his strength fails him imme-
> diately. He is like the shipwrecked sailor, who has
> swum for a very long time—whether furiously or
> calmly, whether the great, rhythmic thrusts of his
> arms and legs came to him instinctively or with the
> help of training—for the momentum and the reality
> of the catastrophe had seized and propelled him.
> Then, suddenly, it dawns on him that he is alone,
> swimming all alone in the vast ocean. All at once, at
> the very moment he becomes conscious of his sit-
> uation, his strength leaves him; all he can do is let
> himself drown. All the drama resides in this reversal
> of perspective—*de jure,* always possible; *de facto,*
> always and at every moment effectible. (DME,
> 122–23 [translation modified])

The event here is neither the shipwreck nor the drowning
but the reversal of the point of view, which is to say, an abrupt
transformation on the swimmer's plane of existence: he is no
longer the same. A radical change takes place in him. He is no
longer the thoughtlessly raging swimmer he was a moment
before—just as the phantom lost the desire for revenge that had
been the reason for his existence. From an architectonic point
of view, the appearance of this new perspective displaces his
center of gravity. There is also the framework of ordinary events,
of course—ordinary in the sense that they do not introduce any
new point of view into the psyche. Like the child's mother, we

see nothing out of the ordinary and have nothing special to do, other than to continue pursuing the same existence.

But certain privileged instants rip this framework apart, resonating in their depths with a profusion of virtualities that constitute the sketch or the promise of a more real existence.[6] "You believe yourself to have found your moment, your climactic instant. But it is the moment that posits *you*, according to the manner in which it is lived for itself and raised to the incandescence of its own reality" (AA, 125).[7] There is an instantaneity of the revelation that springs forth beyond the history of psyches. An eternity rises up, and, from the perspective of this eternity, everything instantly falls into place. This is Souriau's anti-Bergsonism. He isn't interested in duration as a long-term synthesis that gathers in upon itself but in the supreme, formal instant, in the revelation that decides everything, the revelation we know will never fall back into the past because it is already establishing our eternal future.[8] The privileged moments Souriau speaks of, those radiant moments of reality, are themselves events.

Some events are considerable because they *create a soul* in the psyche, which is to say, they give it the "principle of an enlargement," the need or ambition for a more real existence. Such events produce a distension: a distension that is constitutive of the soul itself, tearing the psyche between its base and the summits it can just barely make out, between its ordinary states and its "sublime" moments, between its profane life and its sacred instants, and so on—a distension that establishes the psyche's potential "grandeur," or at least determines the scope of its soul. Fall, elevation, distention—the soul is created alongside the appearance of new dimensions in the psyche. In this sense, there really is a "grandeur of the soul," though this doesn't refer to any particular nobility; it merely measures the distension between various points of view within the psyche. It's because the psyche's ordinary perspective gets overturned that the soul is created within it; the psyche doesn't simply possess a soul but really must *make it exist* as a new dimension of itself.

• • •

Generally speaking, there's soul as soon as we perceive, in some existence, something incomplete or unfinished, demanding a "principle of enlargement"—in short, the sketch of something greater, something more accomplished, capable of augmenting the reality of that existence. We attribute a soul the moment such a distension is introduced into a being. Take the case of the dreadful woman Souriau discusses in *Avoir une âme*: she is unkempt, she is an alcoholic, and she pays no attention to her young child, who is playing by her side. There we have a first "psychic theme," a continuous note that corresponds to the "tonic" of her psyche and determines the general tonality of her existence. But then, in a surge of tenderness, the woman takes the child in her arms and, in a soft voice, sings it a lullaby that seems to come from another world. A different tonality is expressed in this case: no longer the tonic but the "dominant." Her psyche opens onto a different dimension; and "the entire picture is grasped, if only indistinctly, in this single psychic gesture . . . the gesture of maintaining, within oneself, the strict separation and opposition of these two parts of the world" (AA, 131; cf. DME, 168). In this case, we are no longer dealing only with a psyche but with a soul. This isn't to say that the soul corresponds to a movement of spiritual elevation—as opposed to a down-to-earth psyche. The soul isn't one of the poles but the principle of the gap that both separates and relates them. It measures the distance between a *minimum* and an *extremum,* as well as the harmonic relation between the two. It is the gesture that instaurs in the psyche a distance in relation to itself. "Do we not all obtain the measure or maybe the measurable scope of our souls through a sort of gesture of internal distension?"[9]

If what we call a "soul" is the principle of distension between a reality and its virtualities, then every reality can have a soul, not only human psyches. An observer can "attribute" a soul to the psyche of the alcoholic mother, but souls can also be discovered *where there are no psyches*—in vegetables, in minerals, in any fragment of existence whatsoever. This has nothing to do with some sort of animism, no more than it has anything to do with a process of identification or projection. On the contrary, it may be when all projection and identification become impossible that communication is established, in a living and populous solitude. We leave the world of human psyches to enter into communication with nonhuman or infrahuman worlds. When Marguerite Duras invokes the solitude that accompanies the act of writing, she interrupts herself to describe the death of a fly—and it's as if she were saying that that's exactly what the act of writing is: creating a soul for the fly as it struggles against its death.[10] Using Souriau's terms, we would say that the insignificant insect (tonic) is raised to a sort of epic destiny (dominant), following a "principle of enlargement" produced by the act of writing. By what secret, unspoken communication do we give souls and lives to plants and minerals? Do we have to generalize what François Roustang says of certain lives: "Of the human, it was the inhuman that they knew—ingestion and rejection. Had they identified with their surroundings, they would have perished; so, in order to protect themselves from the inhuman that had formed them, they had to seek refuge in the infra-human or in the not-yet-human (which is nonetheless a condition of the human) of animals, vegetables, and minerals."[11] Making matter live, instauring souls in the heart of matter and its "poignant movements," so as to keep from dying?[12] Either matter begins to live and feel or else everything loses its "soul" and nothing can live anymore. We create souls not only for human psyches but for animals, vegetables, minerals—for all of nature's bodies.

The attribution of a soul can be one of the most puerile, sentimental, and even mawkish of operations; yet it becomes a properly instaurative operation when you're heeding the appeal of an architectonic you're devoted to and raising it to a greater existence. To attribute a soul is to enlarge an existence; the generosity of reading, vision, and affection lies in the fact that they allow us to see the greater and the more intense, to see the presence of a soul in certain realities. Is one ever faithful enough to one's own soul or the soul of a work? If someone attributes too much to us, or too much to someone we find completely idiotic or to something uninteresting, does this mean she's seen something we weren't able to see? Or maybe she saw something different than what the idiot saw who got to it first and immediately ruined it? We might reproach her for

not having seen things as they really are or for having embel-
lished. But it isn't that she fails to see what's really there; she
simply sees something different and is searching for signs of it
or is awaiting its return: she sees a soul. From this point of view,
every promotion of existence appears to be a "victory over the
shadows" and over doubt (DME, 138).

The world of souls is very unstable and fragile. A soul takes
shape and then disappears immediately, as evanescent as a
phenomenon. If philosophy has a task, for Souriau, it isn't to
save phenomena but to save the epiphany, ontophany, the-
ophany, psychophany, and so on within phenomena—all those
evanescent beings, always on the verge of disappearing. "We
perpetually observe, particularly in the psychical order, in-
staurations so quick, so fleeting, that we hardly grasp them. We
therefore sometimes posit momentary souls for ourselves (or
they posit themselves in us), whose rapidity and kaleidoscopic
succession contribute to the illusion of a lesser and weak existence; even though they may be greater and more valuable than
those we instaur daily and with the greatest of ease" (DME, 148).
Psychic life never stops hypostasizing, "entifying," what it perceives, and yet most of the time this consistency gives way to
something else that is just as fleeting. The evanescence of phenomena, the lability of thoughts and of entifications, the quasi-
nonexistence of virtuals—so many fragile, precarious modes of
existence, lining the solid and organized world of things.
    All these virtual or potential realities still only form a shadow
play, "more or less richly colored screens, equally capable of
concealing a dreadful void as they are of masking a perspective" (IP, 353). But then how do we know that we aren't just chas-
ing chimeras? For an instant, you glimpsed virtualities striving
for a greater reality—but how can you be sure they're worth the
effort? After all, haven't we all believed, at one time or another,
that we've really "grasped an idea," only to find out later that
it wasn't ultimately all that important? How do you know that
you've made the right choice, that you haven't devoted hours,
days, or years to a project that would ultimately prove vain?
This is the "ontological" force of virtuals. Fragile as they are,

they have the power to disturb the order of the real. What had been real ceases to be real, and what hadn't yet been real becomes real. As in the case of the phantom or the swimmer, a question is enough to turn a perspective on its head, enough for a plane of existence to break apart or collapse. Virtuals have a problematizing force. A problem's force doesn't come from its internal tension but from *the uncertainty it introduces into the (re)distribution of reality.* We enter into a zone where we no longer know what should be considered real. A new perspective bursts onto the scene, disrupting the order of a given plane of existence and displacing the center of gravity of existences.

But, then, how do we know? How can we be sure that one perspective or another isn't illusory? There's no way of knowing in advance. For Souriau, the only solution is to follow the indications of certain virtuals (and to be able to sacrifice others). We run a risk each time. "If we want to see . . . more beautiful kingdoms opened up in [their] depths—we have to make them, not just imagine them. Let us conquer them! But we will not conquer them simply by reaching out, nostalgically, toward the confused dream we have of them. If this conquest never occurs, [we] will simply have to greet them from afar with a wave of the hand, never breaking stride: they are mirages" (IP, 353). To leave the world of shadows, we must then "conquer" new realities. This isn't to say that our problems come to an end there. While we no longer need to ask ourselves if we've made the right decision, the problem remains, for we must constantly respond to the "demands" of the virtuals. Will we be able to give them the radiance and reality they deserve? How will we lead a work to a full possession of itself? The passage from one mode of existence to another is always problematic (what isn't working in my life? what is this first draft, this sketch missing? where is this feeling of a lack of reality coming from? etc.)—no less so than wanting to bring two distinct modes of existence together.[13] It is a matter of making virtuals exist otherwise, of giving bodies to phantoms, in short, of making a being pass into existence in a world other than its own. In other words, the ephemeral swarm must become a cosmos.

In this regard, Souriau constantly speaks of "conquest," of possession. We could even say that, for him, the real is defined by possession. If the question of existence concerns modes of being, *the question of possession concerns degrees of reality.* The more an existence is "possessed," the more real it is. *Avoir une âme* is a significant title in this respect. The book opens with a quick description of some modes of possession:

> To have a soul is to possess riches not actually in your possession; it is truly to live certain unreal lives; it is to be greater than yourself . . . ; it is to constitute a substantial universe and to be that universe yourself, though it be made only of in-substantial events, transitive operations, and la-bile phenomenalities. Even the slightest concrete knowledge of men suffices to show that this is the case for them all, though with great proportional variations. Most truly occupy (if we may put it this way) only a meager portion of their cosmic dimen-sion. Some, moreover, are perfectly content with this condition, and with nothing pushing them to go farther, shut themselves up within this little re-gion of themselves. . . . Almost no souls at all. . . . Others are open. To such an extent are they open to the indistinct and the void that they do not occupy or possess anything. Soul, plenty of soul, but soul that is so tenuous, so inconsistent, so vague, and so little grasped that, in reality, it is nothing at all. (AA, 3)

The concept of possession plays a decisive role in Souriau. It measures the reality of an existence. But, in this case, pos-session doesn't entail the appropriation of a good or a being. Appropriation isn't concerned with property *(la propriété)* but with particularities *(le propre)*. When we speak of appropria-tion, we shouldn't use the verb's pronominal voice but its ac-tive voice: to possess isn't to appropriate *(s'approprier)* but to adapt to . . . *(approprier à . . .)*—in other words, to make some-thing exist in its own right *(en propre)*. It is true that Souriau sometimes seems to employ the verb pronominally, as when he asserts that a psyche should take possession of itself. But, in reality, this means that the psyche should devote itself to the potentialities it has perceived as new dimensions of itself (whether those be moral, aesthetic, or political). We shouldn't say that it appropriates them; on the contrary, we have to say that it adapts its existence to these new dimensions. Only in this way do we understand that they produce a new self within the psyche.

In this sense, to appropriate is to give autonomy to something that doesn't exist through itself and that, given its constitutive incompleteness, *is in need of another* in order to exist more greatly or differently.[14] We say that a virtual "possesses itself" when it acquires an autonomous reality that expresses its architectonic (or its intrinsic point of view) and allows it to maintain itself, by itself, in existence: the completed work. But, for this to happen, it will have to go through a creator, who will grant it access to this new mode of existence. A virtual can only take possession of itself if it finds a mediator or intercessor to give it autonomy. It is a sort of parasitism or symbiotic relationship. The virtual needs a host to exist. Conversely, a creator only ever creates through being the host of virtualities.

Virtuals are like the memories that perform their "wild phantasmagoric dance" in "the night of the unconscious" in Bergson.[15] In his article on dreams, Bergson, following Plotinus, describes memories as a cloud of souls, hovering up above living bodies. They wait to be drawn in by a body that resembles them and responds to their aspirations; they yield to it, let themselves fall, and pass into existence. There is something vampiric about memories. Just as the soul seeks a body, the memory seeks a sensation that resembles it in order to come back to life. "The phantom memory, materializing itself in sensation which brings it flesh and blood, becomes a being which lives a life of its own."[16] Perhaps it's wrong to view Bergson's theory of memory as idealism; instead, we should regard it as a vampirism, like a sort of *élan spectral* that doubles the famous *élan vital.*[17]

The situation is analogous in Souriau: the virtuals are awaiting the process that will give them the autonomy they lack and will allow them to exist on their own, in and for themselves, finally complete. That's the only problem: how to make these virtuals autonomous? By what process? Souriau gives the process a name: it is the *anaphor*. "What we call an anaphor is the determination of the being as a continuous heightening of reality; and anaphoric promotions are the operations that directly concern the promotion of the instaured being toward its patuity" (IP, 10n). It's a question of bringing a virtual from its quasi-nonexistence toward a more manifest reality, or, following Souriau's own terminology, of leading it from the obscure depths, where it remains in the state of a sketch, to the clear light of completion. As its definition states, the anaphor is a process of intensification.[18] "Each new informing is the law of an anaphoric stage. Each anaphoric gain is the reason behind a newly proposed informing" (DME, 129).

Sometimes the intensification takes place while remaining on the same plane of existence, and sometimes it requires bringing together two planes whose modes of being are radically distinct. A plurimodal being is one in which several modes conjoin.[19] Things and psyches are on one plane of existence, virtuals and lucid points on another. The alcoholic's habits are on one plane, the heavenly lullaby on another. A conversation over dinner is on one plane, the seed of a story on another. These are like deep rifts in Being, each bearing witness to the incompletion of the two planes that border it. The anaphor travels across and reduces the distance separating these planes. It conjoins them by leading them to a mutual completion: a sculptor begins *both* with a lump of clay *and* with a virtual project—and *at the same time as* she develops the contours of the clay's form, the virtual project is continuously taking shape on a different plane. At the outset, the real and the virtual are equally undetermined, neither being any more than a sketch.[20] It falls to the anaphoric process to determine them: one in the other, one through the other. The anaphor is the process of "the determination of a being" through the "continuous heightening of reality," up to the point at which the distance separating the real and the virtual has been totally—or nearly totally—abolished. "The distance is constantly diminishing: the work's progression is the progressive coming together of its two existential aspects: the to-be-made and the made. The moment the final touch of the chisel is made, the distance is abolished. It is as if the molded clay is the faithful mirror of the work to-be-made, which in turn has become incarnate in the lump of clay. They are nothing other than one and the same being" (DME, 236). The image of the mirror should not, however, lead us to believe that the lump of clay is molded in the image of the work, as if the latter preexisted its own realization.[21] In reality, the work has no image, or rather, its image takes shape over the course of the work's own creation (DME, 236).

It remains the case that this process is under constant threat of failure and that the distance between the two planes is never fully abolished. One might say that every work is simultaneously a failure and a success.[22] So be it: but to what extent? How long should we keep at it, adding on and cutting away? Don't we risk going too far and ruining the whole thing, justifying "the fear of spoiling the work that is already almost satisfactory with a last-minute mistake" (DME, 237)? These questions aren't concerned with the finishing touches and final details but with the very completion of the work, which we risk leaving in ruins each time we decide to give it one last touch.[23] We perpetually run the risk of "losing the anaphoric thread" (IP, 314). Will we be able to respond adequately to the exigencies of the virtuals? Will we be able to give them the realities they deserve? And how do we begin? We have seen that virtuals, with their problematizing force, never stop posing such questions to us. They accompany our acts of "anaphoric promotion" and make every anaphor a process of experimentation.

To experiment is to try as best as possible to respond to questions that remain ever unformulated. Only in responding are we able to know which question was posed. "The work awaits us, and if we fail to meet it, this does not mean that the work failed to meet us. If we do not give the proper response, it falls apart immediately, departs, returns to the distant limbo from which it began to emerge. For it is in this cruelly enigmatic way that the work questions us, and in this way that it responds to us: 'You were wrong'" (DME 233). The work is a sphinx, but a sphinx to whom we must offer answers without even knowing the nature of the question we're responding to. We have no other choice than to explore the dimensions of the virtual by trial and error, through the false starts and uncertain advances that make the anaphor a permanent experimentation. Each stroke, each phrase, each gesture is like a "proposition of existence" to which the two planes consent—or don't—depending on their respective demands. "At each moment, with each of the artist's actions, or rather *as a result of* each of the artist's actions, [the work under construction] can live or die" (DME, 229).

5

Of Instauration

What exactly does the act of instauration consist in for Souriau? *Instauration* is not synonymous with *anaphor*. *Anaphor* designates the process of intensification by which an existence gains in reality, while *instauration* designates the operation by which an existence gains in "formality" or solidity. Souriau prefers this term to terms like *production* or *creation*, which he judges to be too ambiguous (IP, 73n). Instauration consists in founding the existence of a being, as when one establishes an institution, a ceremony, or a ritual. To create is to institute or *formalize* (IP, 73n). And to formalize is to make the architectonic that is enveloped in the virtual being, still in an "implex" state, pass into existence; it is to unfold the structure. In this sense, we can see why it is less an issue of creating than of instauring. "From a certain point of view, man does not create anything. Nor even does nature create anything. The blossoming of the bud does not create the rose. All of its material and causal conditions were there. The form alone is new. The novelty is immaterial and, naturally, the immaterial alone is new" (IP, 73–74). It's just as Nathalie Sarraute says: she doesn't create the "tropisms," since she already finds them in Flaubert, Dostoevsky, or Virginia Woolf, but she formalizes them differently; she gives them a new "formality" through a new type of story.[1]

It's the well-known question of precursors discovered after the fact. It is true that great works create their own precursors, but what's actually "lacking" in the precursor is the successor's

formalization of the work. Certain aspects are there, but they remain in an embryonic or "implex" state, as if the author hadn't
yet fully explored their potential. Instauration, in this sense, is
the unfolding of "an architectonic that orders, structures, and
consequently distinguishes the initial elements, rather than
leaving them in a state of mutual implication and syncretic
compenetration; and this architectonic outlines other riches,
too, many of which did not exist in the world initially" (IP, 389).
Through this distinction, existences gain, at once, in extension,
in structure, and in consistency—just as a painting, through its
own unfolding, conquers the equilibrium that will make the
colors and lines composing it hold together. Existences acquire
a formal armature that institutes them more than it constitutes
them.

This can be seen through an example drawn from the work
of Eugène Dupréel, whose thought is very close to Souriau's on
this point. Dupréel analyzes the notion of convention in the
social field in order to respond to the question, how is a social group constituted? He describes a first moment in which a
number of individuals form a group on the basis of a common
inclination. This initial group is still so fragile that the individuals still can't count on one another with assurance. No habit,
ritual, or rule has been acquired; it is merely the repetition of a
single novelty. The accord remains implicit and is hardly "consolidated." Then comes the moment of convention, properly
speaking, in which the group becomes "formally responsible,
armed with an explicit rule."[2] Habits are contracted, rituals are
created, rules are laid down. Dupréel thus defines convention
as the result of a consolidation or as a system of such consolidated results. Yet what gives the convention its solidity is its formal character.[3] In a sense, the convention doesn't create anything, since the group already existed, if only informally. But, in
another sense, it does create something new. It creates the "formality" of the convention, which is to say, a consolidation such
that the group is "from then on sustained by something more
determined and also more internal: a formal arrangement of
individual dispositions."[4] The convention is the unfolding of
the architectonic that governs the ensemble of relations be-

tween individuals. For Dupréel, as for Souriau, the formal is the reason behind consistency.

The example Souriau favors is that of philosophical instauration—though, in truth, philosophy isn't just one example among others, since philosophies only do one thing: instaur cosmoi.[5] Every philosophy is a cosmological instauration. "The philosopher sifts and purifies chaos. He arranges it. He seeks to make a world from it once more, shattering the old frameworks for the sake of a new cosmicity" (IP, 51). Philosophers also begin with an informal base, which they then guide toward the highest formality. Philosophical discourse "goes from a minimum, undetermined being, simple *entium entitas*, to fully determined being, completely fulfilled and unfurled, which is the *maximum* of being" (IP, 93). The instaurative act, the properly philosophical "gesture," is this new organization of existences, the network of relations that they gradually establish, and the manner in which they mutually limit and consolidate one another in a cosmos (IP, 402).[6] Philosophers can't just stick to the microcosms revealed through the "blessed instants or ardent minutes" (IP, 394) we described a moment ago. "It is no longer a matter of going straight for the acute, momentary consolidation of an instant, but of instauring oneself along with the others in a rich and complex nexus" (IP, 395). It's a matter of drawing a cosmos out of the chaos and of giving it a solid base.

This isn't to say that Souriau renounces perspectivism—on the contrary. Each cosmos is the expression of a point of view. "You determine a cosmos toward a particular reality. You make it a singular cosmos, different from all others. You posit a cosmos that is not simply being, seen from a certain angle . . . but is posited by a specific instauration, in which you posit yourself, as well. The worlds of Saint Augustine, Spinoza, and Hegel *are not the same worlds*" (IP, 334). Each philosophy is subjected to "the law of the point of view." But the point of view here is not "the author's"; it is the structural—or formal—principle of all philosophy, which organizes the cosmos according to a perspective that is determined gradually.[7] The point of view doesn't preexist what it organizes any more than what it organizes preexists it; the two develop together. "Here, *the point of view is intrinsic*; the work carries with it, in itself and through its own architectonic, this determination of the point of view" (IP, 247). Souriau even believes it would be possible to enumerate all the invariants of this structure and then, perhaps, to put forth a definition of philosophy itself.[8] Here we rediscover the various characteristics of his philosophy: pluralism, perspectivism, and formalism.

What are these invariants? First, there is the law of the point of view, which one could call the law of *determination* or *decision*. It is the order that follows the unfolding or construction of a cosmos and the decisions this necessarily entails at each stage of the work. For not everything can be included in a cosmos, no matter how vast it may be; possibles must be sacrificed constantly.[9] Next, there is the law of significant *opposition*, which organizes philosophies according to a central polarity (the Same and the Other in Plato, thought and extension in Descartes, the thing in itself and the phenomenon in Kant, duration and space in Bergson, etc.). These are the internal dualities that are necessary for philosophies to be constituted. This law is the sign that philosophies have souls in the sense we defined earlier. They are animated by an internal distention, with tonics and dominants. Their capacity to be pulled in different directions gives the measure of their soul's grandeur, their scope (IP, 296). Which oppositions will they be able to fit into their cosmos without it breaking apart?

Following logically is the law of *mediation*, which consists in filling the space between the opposing poles, as when Delacroix adds a touch of pink between a yellow and a blue that oppose one another too severely (IP, 298). It isn't a matter of reconciling the contraries but rather of creating intermediary, mixed, or median beings to populate the intervals. Perhaps the most exemplary case is that of Pascal, who created a permanent disequilibrium by multiplying the perspectival oppositions (the two infinities, wretchedness and greatness, etc.) and who needed a center of reference to give this vertigo a solid base: Christ as the supernatural median point—the central figure of a world deprived of a center.[10] To these three laws must still be added the law of dynamic *evasion* or of conclusion (which introduces a torsion by which a work escapes its own completion and works in a dimension of a different order: a strange dimension that isn't included in it and yet prevents it from withdrawing back into its own perfection—this is, perhaps, the unwritten part that prolongs each philosophy) and the law of philosophical *destruction* (which entails the destruction of old concepts, coming from different philosophical constellations).[11]

These laws (determination, opposition, mediation, evasion, destruction) correspond to formal "gestures," which—as Souriau's examples borrowed from the history of philosophy show—are filled in by particular forms and contents in various ways. The anaphor is submitted to these laws as soon as it seeks to instaur a cosmos and consolidate its parts. The more a philosophy progresses—and this is true of all other works, as well—the more urgent the question of consolidation becomes; for, paradoxically, the edifice becomes more fragile. "Each new operation involves a more immediate and more concrete risk: the risk of losing the anaphoric thread and of discovering that what had been coming together gradually was now undone, scattered, or even destroyed by the error. . . . The artist knows such anxieties well" (IP, 314). The formal principle governs all the forms of the work, all the way up to the final detail, and assures its solidity.

Instauration provides a base. To instaur is not, however, to ground. We aren't dealing with the same "gesture." To ground is to lead all beings back toward a preexisting source, toward a source from which truth or intelligibility derives, just as light derives from the sun. In itself, a grounding is neither true nor intelligible; but as the source of all truth and intelligibility, it is greater than either. As such, it is inseparable from a form that it imposes upon that which it grounds. To be grounded is to have your thoughts, your judgments, and your statements submitted to the form of the true or of the intelligible. The grounding imposes a preexisting Form (when it is transcendent) or dictates its a priori Conditions (when it becomes immanent). In the one case, it imposes a form of truth; in the other, it dictates conditions of veridicality. It doesn't matter here whether the submission takes place through imitation, participation, or conditioning. The important thing is that the grounding gives what is grounded a legitimacy and a form that it wouldn't have had without it.

For grounding is not only the source of truth or intelligibility—it is also the source of legitimacy. Not only does it provide the form of the true or intelligible but it also grants rights: it bestows legitimacy upon the existences that deserve it. This is the mark of its "goodness." How could it not be "good" when it legitimizes the most deserving beings, when it illuminates them and guides their conduct? In this respect, it has the force of a law; and this force is exerted over the grounded, which twists, bends, and turns toward the grounding like a sunflower toward the sun. The quantity of legitimacy received depends upon the greater or lesser submission to the form that the law demands. Conversely, everything that escapes the action of the grounding must, in view of its very manner of being, be deemed illegitimate, which is to say, lacking the right to exist. For the grounding doesn't judge beings so much as manners of being.

How, then, is instauration distinguished from grounding? The grounding preexists, by right, the act that nonetheless posits it; it is external or superior to what it grounds, while instauration is immanent to what it instaurs. *Instauration has no support other than its own gesture,* nothing preexists it—whence Souriau's philosophy of "gestures." In other words, to ground is to make preexist, while to instaur is to make exist, though to make exist in a certain manner—(re)invented each time.[12] "To exist is always to exist in some manner. To have discovered a manner of existing, a special, singular, new, and original manner of existing, is to exist in your own manner" (IP, 366). Existences no longer receive light from an external source; rather, they produce their own over the course of the anaphoric process they trace, from their obscure depths to their luminous summits. It may seem confusing that, in *L'Instauration philosophique,* Souriau sees an instaurative gesture in the grounding act. But this is because the preexistence of the grounding needed first to have been posited, needed to have been instaured in a "gesture." That's what makes philosophy an "art" for Souriau. At the origin of each system lies a great gesture, which deploys its architectonic.[13] Philosophers are the creators of necessary preexistences.

If these gestures are so important, it isn't only because they instaur new modes of existence but also because it is through them that rights are created. It is not an external foundation or grounding but the scope of such gestures that allows a mode of existence to lay claim to its legitimacy. A mode of existence justifies itself by itself—or, rather, it is justified by the immanent gesture that heightens its reality. If Souriau prefers the terms institute and instaur—which belong as much to a philosophy of rights as they do to a philosophy of art—it is because certain existences claim the right to a different manner of being, which would make them more real: "thus, every being posits itself in proportion with and owing to its intrinsic right to be" (IP, 402). Instauration is the assertion and promotion of this right. It is the legitimization of a manner of occupying space-time. Once again, this legitimacy no longer rests upon an external or superior grounding; each existence conquers it through a heightening of its own reality. It is conquered as an existence affirms and deploys its architectonic; it is enriched with determinations and gains in "lucidity."

Consequently, to instaur is to become something like the advocate for these still incomplete existences—their spokesperson *(porte-parole)* or, better yet, their existence-bearer *(porte-existence)*. We support their existences as they support ours. We make *common cause* with them, provided we listen to the nature of their demands, as if they were calling out to be developed, extended, and, in short, rendered more real. To hear these demands, to see what remains incomplete in these existences, is to take their side. And that means entering into the point of view of a manner of existing, not only in order to see the way that it sees but also in order to give it a greater existence, to heighten its dimensions or to make it exist otherwise. "Art and philosophy have it in common that they both aim to posit beings, beings whose existence is legitimized through itself, through a sort of radiant demonstration of a right to existence, which is affirmed and confirmed by the objective radiance, by the extreme reality of the instaured being" (IP, 67). Souriau sees artists, philosophers, and scientists as advocates for fragile existences, for all those existences demanding to exist in another mode or to conquer more reality.

If Souriau always comes back to phenomena on the verge of existing, it's because we usually don't grant them sufficient importance. Perhaps he is addressing beings whose existence is never assured, beings that are deprived, in one way or another, of the right to exist? If he often returns to the question "What is the art of philosophy as *ars magna?*" it's precisely because philosophy is capable of instauring beings of thought—as is evidenced by the many entities it has created: Plato's Ideas, Aristotle's substance, Descartes's *cogito*, Leibniz's monades, and so on. The philosopher's plea (though the same can be said of all creators) is always the same: despite these appearances, despite this apparently insignificant thing, there is a soul, there is the grandeur of a soul, there is an entity.

It all lies in this: becoming real. And to become real is to become legitimate, it is to see your own existence confirmed, consolidated, and sustained in your very being. We know that the surest way of undermining an existence is to act as though it didn't have any reality. Not even going to the trouble of refuting it, simply ignoring it. In this sense, to make exist is always to make exist in the face of ignorance or disregard. We always have to defend the subtle against the unrefined, the background against the din of the foreground, the rare against the ordinary, everything whose mode of knowledge has the crudest ignorance as its correlate. "The common—worst of all!" wrote Henry James.[14] It might be surprising that there are philosophies of the ordinary, but it shouldn't surprise us that they deny everything that falls outside of their ruts.

This is because doubting an existence isn't only provisionally suspending the reality of a being but also calling into question the well-foundedness of its existence. To doubt is to call a right into question. It isn't so much the existence of a thing as its right to exist that we doubt. That's why doubt is both ineffective and devastating: ineffective, because it doesn't prevent the thing from existing; devastating, because it deprives it of reality (which is to say, of its right to exist). In Souriau, doubt ceases to appear as a purely methodological operation, as it does in Descartes or Husserl, and instead acquires the performativity of an accusative judgment or an indictment: it reduces certain existences to a spectral state by depriving them of reality.

Consequently, every existence must fight against this doubt in order to posit itself.

This can be seen in Souriau's description of the arrival of spring. He chooses the moment when spring has yet to appear in full force precisely because at that point it still needs to triumph over winter's presence. "How I have waited for spring! I almost doubted it was still possible that it would come. If now it triumphs, it is a victory over doubt and absence. If it is said that *the beauty of the world* is not a meaningless phrase, this is because the arrival of spring testifies against that doubt. Its testimony therefore appeals to and presupposes the doubt itself. A force finally freed, a being finally come to pass, it is upon the obscure ground of all that absence that it stands out" (DME, 135). Each privileged moment possesses not only a formal armature through which colors, lines, and lights enter into a delicate composition but also an affirmative force that testifies in favor of that moment's existence and in favor of "the beauty of the world."

Here we reach what may be the essence of art for Souriau: to create is, above all, *to bear witness.* Creators, including philosophers, are witnesses.[15] Each work is the work of a witness (which should not be confused with its author). "It is not a question of an incidental witness, nor of a witnessing reader or reciter, but of the ideal and internal witness that the work institutes, so that it may be established in relation to its own self. Any soul coming into contact with the work will have to identify with this ideal, internal witness to a greater or lesser extent; not even the soul of the author will escape this requirement" (IP, 252). We can see why Souriau defines a point of view as a "testimonial point." It's because each creator of existence testifies in favor of what she creates as if she were making a *pro domo* defense speech. Each of her "works" supports the cause of new entities. We always testify in favor of the "beauty of the world," in favor of its intelligibility and "cosmicity," by revealing new beings within it. You need an art to make others see what you've seen. In this sense, to show is *to act as a witness.* At one point or another, every person is witness to a moment of splendor or truth, fleeting though it may be.

But only those who decide to testify in favor of those beauties

or truths, only those who make common cause with the "privileged" moments or with the modes of existence whose reality
they hope to promote, become advocates. Every appearance,
for Souriau, is always an appearing before or a summons, not
only because nothing ever appears completely on its own but
because we are always the witness or advocate in an ongoing
case.[16] Take, for instance, the example of the man who, in the
dark, comes into contact with a tree whose existence he knows
perfectly well in broad daylight: "I can strike this tree, so I do: I
strike it. I make it demonstrate its presence. . . . It is a testimony,
wrenched from the universal presence, that forced it to appear
in the guise of a tree's bark against my hand. It was forced to
inscribe itself in the frame my murky and troubled mind—that
frail being—held out to it. And my mind is bolstered and but-
tressed by the testimony. It is established in it and with it" (IP,
239).

The tree and the man share a *common cause* in the sense
that they mutually lend support to one another's existence. The
man supports the tree's existence, while the tree supports the
existence of the man and his mind, that "frail being." This isn't
at all a case of corporeal reversibility but rather of mutual edification and the production of a real consistency between two
beings. Existing and making exist participate in a single process, which makes instauration a necessarily mutual process—
the process by which Cervantes and Don Quixote, Leibniz
and the monadology, Thompson and the electron, and so on
are constructed mutually, each according to its own mode of
existence. Each testifies for the soul of the other. In Souriau,
a soul never exists alone; it exists by making other souls exist.
And these others exist, correlatively, by making the first exist.
You only exist yourself by making yourself the advocate of other
souls—including your own, understood as the self-expansion
to which you aspire. You only become real by making other
existences more real. "In the passing moment itself, my only
means of clinging to being and of realizing myself is to realize
this moment in myself, with myself; to sink my teeth into the
moment that is and to force it, from within itself, to shout out
its name" (IP, 369).

This is an essential point that Souriau insists upon: the solidarity of the work and the creator, such that each makes the other exist. The work heightens its reality, while the creator expands her soul through the perspective that the work opens up for her. The soul is expanded by the work, while the work is brought into existence for and through itself—these are two "monumentalities," which, in the best of cases, attain complete possession of themselves, as happens in the case of things. Instead of a symbiotic relationship, we have seen that Souriau invokes a veritable spiritual parasitism—but he does so in order to emphasize the autonomy at which the work will ultimately arrive. "Should we say that Dante used the experiences of his exile in the *Divine Comedy*, or that it was the *Divine Comedy* that needed Dante's exile? When Wagner becomes enamored of Mathilde, is it not *Tristan* that needs Wagner to be in love? . . . All the great works grasp the man in his entirety, and the man is no longer anything but the servant of the work, that monster in need of nourishment. Scientifically speaking, we can speak of a veritable parasitism of the work with respect to the man."[17]

The work begins as the phantom that haunts the artist's soul; but then the relationship is reversed and the artist becomes the pale phantom of an increasingly autonomous, radiant, and fully real work—just like in Henry James's novella *The Private Life*. Once again, this is the sign of a profound conception of *possession*. To have a soul is to possess oneself or to aspire to the possession of oneself, to aspire to the virtualities that accomplish us and make us autonomous. But it is also to be possessed by this perspective, in the sense of being haunted by another soul. Possession only ever has to do with souls. Even the most staunch materialist knows, you only ever possess, and are only ever possessed by, a soul—the very soul you attribute to things and beings. Only spiritualism can think possession.

If there's an author who could be said to be close to Souriau, it would be Hofmannsthal, with his sensitivity to the kind of existential pluralism Souriau speaks of, and especially to the least assured, most unassuming existences, which, for him, are a sort of injustice belonging to every era. "This is the secret, it is one of the secrets from which our age is formed: everything in

our age is present and at the same time not present in all of you.
Our age is full of things that seem alive and are dead, and full of
those that count as dead and are altogether alive. . . . This age
is full to the point of illness with unrealized possibilities, and at
the same time it is rigidly full of things that seem to exist only
because of their mere existence, even though they no longer
have life in them."[18] It is a sort of injustice belonging to every
age that life should fill the world with soulless (and irrelevant)
things, and yet be, at the same time, rich with an abundance
of unrealized possibilities. Hofmannsthal observes that there is
an instability, malady, or "chronic vertigo" that creates a state
of permanent discord among the modes of existence. Whoever
hopes to give more reality to the neglected existences shares in
this discord. She is like the phantom, the specter. "And so the
poet is present where he does not seem to be and is always in a
different place than he is thought to be. Strangely, he lives in the
house of the age, under the stairs, where everyone must pass by
and no one notices him."[19]

From this point of view, Hofmannsthal's *The Letters of the
Man Who Returned* is quite astonishing. They are the letters of
a man who returns to Germany after twenty years of travels and
exile, throughout which Germany had played the role of his na-
tive land. It had been like the spiritual double of all the lands
he crossed: every event he experienced—whether in Spain, in
Montevideo, or elsewhere—was interwoven with this strange,
spiritual Germany he carried with himself. The voyager and
his shadow. He was "in Germany all those times, and wherever,
whether in Uruguay or in Canton or, as recently, on the islands,
something struck [his] soul."[20] But now that he is back in Germany, he can no longer find this personal Germany and feels
himself to be profoundly exiled, deterritorialized. After that, everything begins to lose its reality and vitality, as if it had all been
stricken with some imperceptible falsity. The landscapes are
just bad décor, and the people are all fakes. He is surrounded
with disappointment. The voyager no longer knows "what
these people are living for." "And I haul the great Germany and
the Germans of today before the judgement seat of these child-
ish notions, from which, at heart, I cannot free myself, and I
see that they do not live up to my standards, and I cannot get

over it."[21] Their existences can no longer be justified, and as a result, each of their gestures is shot through with unreality—even though all the strangers he had met on his travels had been all the more real for being doubled by his tie to a dreamt and idealized Germany. Rarely has the double experience of return—the moment when you discover that you never left completely, even though it's now impossible to return—been described with such force. It isn't only the passersby crossing paths with him in the street: even the clothes stand and wash basin of his hotel room are marked with the same unreality. Victim of a "sickness . . . of a European nature,"[22] the voyager, upon his return, is a specter among other specters, exploring the theater of shadows and the modal variations described by Souriau.

But the moment of revelation comes at last: the arrival of an exhibition where, thanks to the genius of an unknown painter, the world rediscovers its full reality. Everything that appears upon one of his canvases regains its reality, as if this painter had succeeded in vanquishing all doubts:

> How can I make you understand this, that here, every being—*one being,* every tree, every streak of yellow or virescent field, every fence, every sunken road torn into the stony hill, one being the tin jug, the clay bowl, the table, the heavy cushioned chair—they all held themselves up to me as if newly born from the terrible chaos of Not-living, from the abyss of non-existence, so that I felt—no—I knew how each of these things, these creatures, was born out of a terrible doubt concerning the world, and now covered up with its existence a horrible gorge, a yawning nothingness, for ever! How can I give you even half an idea of how this language spoke into the soul, throwing to me the great justification of these most strange, most inextricable of conditions of my inner being, making me in a second compre-hend what I in unbearable torpor could hardly bear to feel, and what I nevertheless, how strongly I felt this, could not eradicate from myself – and here, an

unknown soul of inconceivable strength, answered
me, answered me with a world![23]

At the end of the letter (which was written in 1901), we learn
that the painter of this "great justification" is Van Gogh. What
is justified here is not so much the states of the voyager's inner
being as it is the existence of things through which his inner
being can exist anew. For the voyager's discovery is that the two
exist in a relation of mutual dependence: we exist through the
support of things, just as we lend support to things that exist
through us, in a mutual edification or instauration. We only
exist by making exist. Or, rather, we only become real by making what exists more real. If things only exist by vanquishing
doubt, if they have this power, how could it fail to communicate itself to those who experience its reality, how could it fail to
awaken in them at that very moment, in a shared justification
of world-making?

One thing is certain: this legitimization never comes from
the subject. How could the subject possibly legitimize what appears to her, when it's *to her* that it appears? What gives her the
right to legitimize an existence? The fact that it appears to her in
particular? What happens in reality is the complete opposite. It
is what she witnesses that grants her this right—or, at least, allows her to claim such a right. It is what we witness that makes
us feel we are justified to . . . *(fondé à . . .)*, which is quite the
opposite of making the Ego a foundation or a ground. Otherwise, we confuse two attitudes: one that feels itself to be important for having seen, and another that feels the importance of
what has been seen. A "witness can have infinitely less reality
than that which establishes it as a witness" (IP, 9). To believe
the contrary is to fall victim to the illusion that, "instead of having to be justified in themselves, those lucid sites of the world,
those monads of singular perfection, would only be justified in
relation to the fully-constituted subjects that experience them,
think them, and comprehend them in their affections."[24]

6

The Dispossessed

Is existence ever a piece of property we possess?
Is it not rather an objective and a hope?

—Étienne Souriau

Anaphor is the process through which an existence attempts
to conquer more reality, while instauration is the gesture with
which it aims to assert its right to exist. The two are inseparable. The intensification of an existence's reality always has as
its correlate the affirmation of its right to exist. And because
this right is no longer bestowed by some sovereign grounding,
it needs to be conquered by other means. But what happens
when one is completely dispossessed of the right to exist in one
mode or another? When there's no longer a way out? You have
the right to exist, of course, but not in this manner, nor in that
one, nor in any other . . . The question is political as much as
it is aesthetic. It's Kafka's question, but also the question of all
those who, in one way or another, are deprived of this right. The
problem of existence is not that of its facticity, its irreducible
contingency, or its absurdity. The problem is more basic: it is a
question of *really* existing.

There is, however, an apparent absurdity in this problem:
how could existence constitute a problem when it is something

irreducibly given? Why seek an entryway into existence when you're already inside? The discussion will clearly remain abstract and futile without the introduction of modal distinctions. Existing with the permanence of a thing, existing as a "*réique*" existence, to use Souriau's term, isn't enough for us to be able to "posit" existence as it would be conceived in relation to a different mode. To think it did would be to miss entirely the distinction between right and fact. You aren't real simply because of the *fact* that you exist; you're only real on the condition that you've conquered the *right* to exist. We can certainly describe existences as being "thrown" into the world or refer to their "being-in-the-world." But what about those existences that haven't found the way in that leads to their "being-in-the-world"? Rather than feeling thrown into the world, they feel as though they've been thrown out of it, expelled by their own reality. Or perhaps the part that's in-the-world no longer belongs to them; perhaps the world has already dispossessed them of it in advance. That's the situation in which Kafka the bachelor finds himself: "I must just take my walks and that must be sufficient, but in compensation there is no place in all the world where I could not take my walks."[1]

The Kafkian bachelor is a man without world, but precisely because he is also a man without family—in the sense that he is incapable of "founding" a family.[2] He isn't at the foundation of anything and can't "found" anything at all. He is the complete opposite of the family father in the famous "Letter to His Father." There the father appears as the incarnation of the figure of foundational authority. He despotically reigns over a vast space-time, which extends far beyond the family circle. "From your armchair you ruled the world."[3] Not only is he in control of every right but he doles them out arbitrarily, according to his whims: the right to speak, the right to marry, the right to think, and so on. The bachelor son is like the symmetrical opposite of the father. If the father is necessarily the family father, then the son is without family, just as necessarily. Lacking both ancestors and descendants, he is destined to be the bachelor.

Or we could also say that the bachelor is a disinherited son. He's alone, without a circle, with no possessions, deprived of even the most basic rights. On the map of the world, he occupies a minuscule, barely visible point. He lives in a space that grows more and more cramped, and time, for him, loses all continuity until it is ultimately reduced to a series of instants. He's so barely real that he can no longer even be sure of having a body. "Since there was nothing at all I was certain of, since I needed to be provided at every instant with a new confirmation of my existence, since nothing was in my very own, undoubted, sole possession, determined unequivocally only by me—in sober truth a disinherited son—naturally I became unsure even to the thing nearest to me, my own body."[4] What's left for the bachelor, then, he who has neither time nor space, neither thought nor language?[5] He lives in a world where he is stripped of every right. Besides, it only makes sense he'd possess nothing himself, when, from his father's point of view, he's such a good-for-nothing!

The only way for the bachelor to recover his rights is for him to take legal action and go to trial. The solution may seem surprising, since we all know that it's impossible to win a trial in Kafka, even—and especially—if you're innocent. If you need to "prove" your innocence, you've already lost. As Titorelli says in *The Trial*, there's no real acquittal or innocence reclaimed; those are only legends. But then why a trial? What can you possibly hope to get out of it? It's because the trial is the only way of escaping the conviction. For as long as it lasts, you aren't guilty, no decision has been made: an ongoing case. You'll certainly be the target of various accusations, but at least you won't be guilty of anything. Hence the "Letter to His Father" as an attempt at a trial or the letters to Felice as an "other trial," in which accusations and self-accusations alternate indistinctly.[6] Indeed, with regard to the "Letter to His Father," Kafka warns Milena, "As you read it, understand all the lawyer's tricks: it is a lawyer's letter."[7]

The trial is therefore both inevitable and interminable. Inevitable, because it has to prevent the accusation from becoming a conviction, interminable, because you can never do more than postpone the conviction; you will never be acquitted. That's the meaning of the indefinite postponement that Titorelli expounds upon in *The Trial*: "The trial doesn't end of course, but the defendant is almost as safe from a conviction as he would be as a free man."[8] And this is equally one of the objectives of the "Letter to His Father." If it's necessary to go to trial, it's because the procedure makes it possible to strip the father of his sovereign position and to suspend his previous convictions. "This terrible trial that is pending between us and you . . . a trial in which you keep on claiming to be the judge, whereas, at least in the main (here I leave a margin for all the mistakes I may naturally make) you are a party too, just as weak and deluded as we are."⁹ It is therefore necessary to become an advocate, in order to counter the arbitrary power of the judge—the man of grounds—who deprives the individual of his rights. Without a doubt, the bachelor remains just as destitute as he is in Kafka's descriptions; but, in becoming an advocate, he at least reclaims the right to think, speak, or write on behalf of the accused—that is, on his own behalf.

In a certain way, we aren't that far from Beckett's characters. There's no question of setting up a Kafka/Beckett parallel, since, from the one to the other, the situation is entirely different. The only point in common is that Beckett's characters are also dispossessed. They've been divested of everything. But, in their case, the dispossession has become an asset, a sort of a priori condition. They no longer demand any rights. "We've no rights anymore? . . . We've lost our rights?—We got rid of them."¹⁰ In Beckett, one is born dispossessed to such an extent that the idea of a trial is devoid of meaning. "I gave up before birth, it is not possible otherwise."¹¹ Since they don't have the means to possess themselves, they instead ask to whom they could possibly belong. Who put them in this situation? Who is responsible for them? What's more: who speaks, who thinks for them, in their heads? Their only possessions are a few paltry objects, which they periodically inventory.

But the great difference, with respect to Kafka, is that this state of dispossession doesn't even cause them to suffer. They have other problems. What distinguishes Beckett's characters and gives them such an immense comic force is their *ambition*. They've truly been stripped of everything, but they nevertheless look forward to something. They aren't entitled to anything, and there isn't anything they're aiming to possess; more often than not, they don't even understand what's asked of them.¹² So, then, what is this ambition of theirs? *They look*

forward to being done with it all. No more talking, no more seeing, no more thinking, no more moving—to be done with it all.
On a good day, this ambition might even make them a bit pre-
sumptuous: "I could die today, if I wished, merely by making
a little effort, if I could wish, if I could make an effort."[13] But
then: they'll never be able to fulfill their ambitions; they don't
even have enough will to want to do so. They never succeed in
shutting their mouths for good, in ceasing entirely to think or to
move. There are always leftover scraps, vibrations, preventing
them from being done with it, keeping the end from ever ending. "For to end yet again."[14] It's in this sense that they're even
radically dispossessed: they can't even decide to be done with
it. They're no more in control of this decision than of anything
else, and so they go on enduring the gestures, voices, and perceptions that keep disturbing them regardless. They discover
the interminable. But now it isn't the trial that's interminable,
as it was in Kafka, but the end.

Standing in the way of the end are all those leftover entities,
rising up: jolts, shudders, itches, discomforts, scraps of memories, of speech, of forgotten promises, and so on. At first glance,
it seems as though Beckett's universe seeks to attain silence,
immobility, black, gray, or white as ultimate limits. But, in reality, what we discover is that the black is never total, the silence never complete, the immobility never absolute—and his
characters reflect and resonate this situation. Something inex-
orably persists, something we could call vitality if we wanted:
a force that they don't possess but that they themselves belong
to, that imposes a minimum of activity upon them. There are
certainly new modes of existence that appear alongside such
characters; however, the process that instaurs them is no longer anaphoric but catastrophic. The distance is no longer that
between a minimum and an extreme but between a minimum
and nothingness. A principle of reduction is substituted for the
principle of expansion. We no longer rise up, we fall; and it's
in falling—through waste, decline, and ridicule—that new, almost nonexistent, nearly null entities appear. "Faint light in the
room. Whence unknown. None from the window. No. Next to
none. No such thing as none."[15] But for this to be achieved, we
need to be sufficiently destitute, we have to have lost enough.

How are we affected if not by shudders, starts, and murmurs? How are we to reach those zones where nothing and no one will challenge our claims?

The attempt to populate zones deemed barren or hostile to the senses with new entities is, without a doubt, a tendency that can be found throughout all the arts. But haven't the arts run up against the limit of their possibilities in their desire to reach pure, abstract qualities? White, black, silence, nothingness— are these ultimate limits that embody the end or quintessence of an art? How do we instaur new beings in these zones if it's true that there is nothing beyond white, black, silence, or void? How many times has the death of an art been announced on the pretext that it has reached its unsurpassable limit? There are many apparent boundaries that have been erected as walls: What music is there beyond Cage and his 4'33" of silence? What painting is there beyond Malevitch's white square on a white background? Beyond Rauschenberg's *White Paintings* or Robert Ryman's monochromes? What images are there after the static shots or black screens of video art? Or after Warhol's *Sleep*? We could go on listing such examples, which are all conceived of as experimental forms in the vicinity of an unsurpassable limit.

But if there's a lesson to be learned from Beckett on the subject of the limit, it's that, far from being unsurpassable, the limit is, on the contrary, unattainable. It can only be grasped if we pass over to its other, *concrete* aspect. But what could possibly be concrete in such a degree zero, in such a state of utter neutrality or lack, of total white, of definitive gray or black? We get the impression that, in such zones, perception has to change its scale. Where certain people will only ever see a pure quality as an abstraction, others will see a surface reflecting the movements and minuscule displacements that are induced by a change of scale in perception itself. The limit is no longer embodied in an abstract quality; it becomes a living, sensitive membrane. André Masson characterized the canvas as an epidermis; but we should say that every medium, every material, is vibratile and that their purpose is to gather even the most minuscule of the limit's vibrations. Everything around it begins to vibrate. It isn't just the ear, skin, or canvas that vibrates; every body vibrates. Cinematographic and video images are themselves animated by minuscule, luminous, or chromatic variations, which their volatile sensitivity can't help but capture. This is not an indication of an imperfection but of the fact that *we are dealing with bodies*, whether physical, technological, musical, pictorial, or what have you.

The first thing to shift our perspective on the limit's abstraction is the presence of bodies. The concrete isn't the materiality of bodies in themselves but the "noise" of their vibrations—like the way the sound of voices, issuing from a loudspeaker that is gradually being submerged in sand, is reduced to an unintelligible vibration in Gary Hill's *Meditations* (1986) or like the parasitism of Nam June Paik's videos. Bodies, including technical and technological bodies, are no longer tools of reproduction or adaptation but recording surfaces and sensitive sensors. They record movements, "noises" at the limit of the audible or visible, making them into something like souls or minds, even when they are mechanized or industrial.[16] It's no longer merely a question of creating souls but of arranging and cobbling together new bodies. If the limit can't be reached, it really is because of bodies. The four minutes and thirty-three seconds of Cage's piece are inseparable from the noises of the concert hall, which constitute the voluminous body of the silence. Regarding *4'33"*, Cage (sounding rather like Beckett) states that it isn't a matter of attaining silence, but that "the ending will approach imperceptibility."[17]

Despite the extinction it approaches, the limit is inseparable from a "noise"—though a noise that can't be reduced to the definition given to it by information theory. Instead of being conceived as something that disrupts the transmission of information, this noise becomes the object of a new conquest: like the "Undersound" Bill Viola speaks of, the constant noise of the world, which absorbs all other sounds and needs to be captured even if it is inaudible and unintelligible. In other words, the change of scale renders the limit inaccessible, because of the microphysical agitation that is revealed in its vicinity. If, on the contrary, we remain on the side of the abstract limit, we eliminate all bodies. We retain only their generality, a pure, monochromatic quality: white, silence, black, absence, and so on.

On the concrete side of the limit, everything is extremely animated: the white is animated by movements, by a vibrant fluttering, as in a snowstorm. So much so that, from this point on, instauration will consist in the creation of sensors, transmitters, and motion detectors. This is the case not only for the cameras people have tinkered with to modify their sensitivity but for all the arts, including the mobile statues that harness the power of the wind, as well as solar, mechanical, and electric energies. Rauschenberg defined his monochromes as "hypersensitive screens," and Cage described them as "airports for the lights, shadows, and particles." Black has its own movements and internal vibrations, as in Soulages, whose compositions capture the lights of the "Outrenoir," beyond black. Like the "Undersound," the Outrenoir is really the moment when black ceases to appear as a uniform quality, instead becoming "a light reflected beyond black, transformed by the night. Outrenoir: black that, in ceasing to be black, becomes a transmitter of clarity, of secret light. Outrenoir: a mental field other than the black."[18] Microphysical reception that makes the black itself become a "mental field" and take on a spiritual life. Capturing vibrations to make matter live, to make colors live for themselves—or, in Souriau's terms, to give them souls.

This isn't to say that there's no more abstraction but rather that abstraction ceases to be an ultimate limit and instead becomes perceptible. What are we to make of that? To grasp, now, not what emerges from the mist but the mist itself as an abstraction immanent to perception. We must imagine, for example, a canvas on which there's nothing to see, not even a smudge or a pattern or any sort, but off of which colors rise like vapors. Maybe that's what happens with Agnes Martin? It's a kind of painting with no object and no form to look at (photographic reproductions can only give us a very faint approximation of this). Her paintings usually present a group of straight, horizontal lines that striate the canvas at regular intervals, like in a school notebook. They form vast charts or grids that are like the picture's degree zero or the "innocense [*sic*] of mind."[19] There's a classicism to which Agnes Martin keeps returning as a point of departure or redeparture.[20] Colors enter into the picture, too: nearly translucent colors, which, more often than not, respect the layout of the lines, following gradations or binary alternations. We could say that the smoothness and the gradation of the lines constitute the conditions for the appearance and the application of color and its chromatic range. Despite the serenity of these paintings, we quickly come to realize that there is something like a struggle between the lines and the colors. We rediscover, in a purified form, the clash that Cézanne reveals between the "stubborn geometry" of nature, which tends to close in upon itself like a fist, and the irradiant force of color.[21]

In Agnes Martin, the eye goes from the line to the color, but, in the end, color always prevails. It frees itself from the line, rises up, and floats like a mist. But then, why the lines? Because without them, we wouldn't see the color breaking free and spreading. As with mist, if you want to grasp its movement, you must first make out the objects it's made disappear. That's what happens with Agnes Martin: we see color still in the process of erasing the lines and becoming ethereal or nebulous. They aren't monochromes, even if at first they appear to be, because monochromes are opaque: there's nothing "behind" their two-dimensionality, even if they have "depth." By contrast, in Agnes Martin, there really is something "behind" the color: the lines that are in the process of disappearing or appearing. Her use of colors gives them a transparency that dematerializes and vaporizes them to the point of abstraction.[22] Only, this abstraction doesn't efface bodies. It's true that the color no longer colors bodies; but that's because color has become a body itself, a transparent, hazy body. Abstraction is the body become pure color or color become immaterial body.

Throughout these examples, we're no longer concerned with an abstract limit that represents the final possibility of an art and erects a wall separating an art from everything foreign to its supposed essence. When the limit becomes concrete, it no longer separates the same things; or, rather, its function is no longer to separate the arts from but, on the contrary, to make them communicate with elements that are foreign to their supposed

essences. It is now generally accepted that painting communi-
cates with nonpainting, literature with nonliterature, theater
with nontheater, dance with nondance, as a condition of their
respective activities. Art becomes *essentially* impure. Noise and
images are introduced into music; photographs, fabric, wood,
and all sorts of materials are introduced into painting and
sculpture; images, hypertext, voice, and cut-ups are introduced
into literature, and so on. All the arts are affected by a "trans-
versality" and by forms of recycling and hybridization that
make them all "multimedia." Works of art are all plurimodal or
transmodal.

Just as Varèse or Cage opens music up to noise, Robert
Ryman can say, in an interview, that white interests him, not
for its own sake, but because it reacts with wood, color, and
light.[23] The white's value lies in its ability to capture elements
that are heterogeneous to it, as Rauschenberg says in his own
way, speaking of his *White Paintings*: "I always thought of the
white paintings as being not passive but very—well, hypersensitive . . . so that one could look at them and almost see how
many people were in the room by the shadows cast, or what
time of day it was."[24] Rauschenberg's oeuvre presents us with
a passage from the white and the erasure (the famous *Erased
de Kooning Drawing*) to the later compositions, which are veritable patchworks, bringing together heterogeneous fragments,
soiled and stained monochromes, with socks, photos, newspaper clippings . . . Maybe this extremely active communication of
elements requires going through the "reduction" we described
above: white, silence, or black as degree zero.

It's like a fall, but one from which we wouldn't have to get
back up again. Would we even be able to get back up again,
anyway? The anaphor literally becomes catastrophic or *cata-
phoric* (in the sense that *ana* designates a movement from the
bottom to the top and *kata* the inverse movement). It's a manner of purging your perception, of cleansing your eyes in order
to rediscover the force of seeing and of showing. If you aren't
going to instaur something, the most you can do is to duplicate,
détourne, or parody—to become a professional in the realms of
"irony" and kitsch. The "catastrophe" is necessary as the limit's
conversion point. It passes from the *terminus ad quem* to the

terminus a quo, where the abstract impossible transforms into a field of potentialities or "pregnancies," to speak like Souriau.[25] Here, again, the reduction isn't meant to reach the pure quality or the essence (eidetic reduction) but permits an opening onto the inessential, which is to say, onto the impure, heterogeneous elements through which experimentation takes place (experimental reduction). Through new architectonics, art becomes the reception and composition of the heterogeneous, rather than ceaselessly driving toward its own supposed essence.

The anaphoric process described by Souriau is certainly inverted here—from promotion to the fall—but it's always a question of doing justice to new entities, of grasping them at the moment of their appearance or disappearance (through the unstable play of possessions and dispossessions). The most striking moments, for Souriau, are those in which a new existence appears, as if released from the mist and needing to heighten its reality. Even when, on the contrary, it's a matter of grasping its dissipation—like in the work of Oscar Muñoz, who works against photographic images, to substitute specters for them. To create holograms, to bring a phantom portrait back to life in a breath or in a reflection, or even to submit photographic images to a play of appearance/disappearance to compromise the instantaneity of the take and its "reality"—to liquify their forms and dissipate them in the white, before making them suddenly reappear from the white as if from a profound amnesia (cf. the series of "protographies"). Muñoz submits the images to an existential modulation where it's no longer a question of anything other than appearing and disappearing—through an exploration of various modes of existence other than that of the fixed image. As Souriau would say, we enter into a world where the solidity of bodies, the sharpness of outlines, and the fixity of images give way to the verbs that affect all the modes of existence: appear, disappear, reappear.

Appendix

Art and Philosophy

Étienne Souriau

If philosophy is spirit's reflection upon itself, it has three principal branches: reflection on science, reflection on art, and reflection on the concrete practice of life (on action, to the extent that it shapes the agent): θεωρεῖν *(theōreîn)*, ποιεῖν *(poieîn)*, πράττειν *(práttein)*.

But, even if we give πράττειν *(práttein)* an eminently moral meaning, there is still too much action in science and art, and too much science and art in action, for this division ever to be entirely satisfying. What is truly essential in this tripartition is the prerogative thought gives to one or another of these three aspects, as when its predilections lead it to consider or to accomplish itself either as having a content, or as leading to the completion of a work, or as concerning the agent from which it proceeds and to whom it is imputed.

In this respect, science is art inasmuch as one considers the ensemble of the data it has gathered to be a work; and action is art to the extent that the agent himself can be the very work his action strives to accomplish. Reciprocally, art is science in that it has a content; and art is action in that it can be attributed to the artist.

Of course, thus understood, the notion of art far exceeds the pure, rich, solid, and, moreover, exemplary—though also narrow—domain of the seven fine arts. But, even when it focuses exclusively upon the narrow and exemplary domain of the fine arts, if the preceding is true, reflection on art is a branch of reflective philosophy that is not only always important but also always necessary, no matter what form of thought its predilections lead it to reflect upon. It is always useful, always legitimate, and sometimes necessary to regard spontaneous thought reflectively from the aesthetic point of view.

However, if philosophy is not reflective, but direct—if philosophy is in name and in fact either the highest form of knowledge, or the *opus majus,* or the agent's advantageous adaptation to the entire problematic of action—then is it still true that two of these three conceptions place art in a position that is outside of and accessory to philosophy's essential preoccupations? We should not accept that this is the case. For the abstraction that separates a philosophy from art (by which I mean the fine arts), even in the case of a philosophy that is technically directed toward a nonaesthetic end, gives only a partial and deformed image of that philosophy, as compared with the living reality of its labor.

Let us seek and enumerate the concrete relations between art and philosophy, starting with the most concrete, and especially with those that appear at once to the historian of philosophy.

The first of these relations is what we might call *epochal symbiosis.*

As useful as it might be to separate the total life of human spirit into distinct strands, so as to present the facts more clearly and to follow the course of its principal branches, such an abstraction from their organic unity is still, ultimately, nothing more than an abstraction. And this abstraction becomes a risk, and then an error, if, forgetting their unity, one goes on to consider the isolated strands as if they were really independent from one another. The same is true on both the individual and collective planes. To write a clear biography of Leonardo da Vinci, it may be useful to separate the artist and the man of science, and to address these two aspects of his intellectual life separately and successively—but that would only be an artifice for the sake of the presentation. Goethe was a poet, an artist, and a biologist. But no one will understand the *Walpurgisnacht* of the second *Faust* who forgets the poet's scientific preoccupations. No one will understand his theory of the transformation of vertebrates who forgets the grand, poetic vision of life that animates and inspires it. The same is true of the collective being we think of whenever we consider the total and authentic unfolding of human thought: it thinks, wants, imagines, suffers, and hopes; it learns, discovers, and calculates; it makes theorems, astronomical systems, physical and chemical discoveries, poems, statues, symphonies, buildings, institutions, and laws. All of that is the varied and multiple evidence of an activity, whose unity, but also whose internal conflicts or divergent intentions, constitute an organic whole. Nothing in it can be isolated from the rest, not even what has been done by an individual. What a strange idea we would have of a philosopher if we presented him as a solitary mind, with only a technical and, as it were, scholastic connection to a small group of predecessors—itself made up exclusively of philosophers!

To be sure, it is useful to remember that Spinoza read Descartes. But it is no less useful to recall that, as a child, he played in the immediate vicinity of Rembrandt's studio.

Can I really understand the *Discourse on the Method* if I ignore or forget that, during the years of Spinoza's childhood when Descartes published this work in Leiden (Spinoza was five years old at the time), not only had Rembrandt just transported the capital of painting from Haarlem to Amsterdam but old Rubens was also still painting (he painted the *Garden of Love* in 1633); Frans Hals, Brouwer (who would die young the following year), and Van Ostade were in full form; in Italy, not only were Galileo and Torricelli living but also Monteverdi; and that same year, in 1637, Venice inaugurated the first public opera house?

Even to suppose (as is certainly false) that Spinoza was ignorant of Rembrandt's work and that Descartes knew nothing of Monteverdi, it would nonetheless be true that Spinoza and Descartes were bound up with a living moment in the spiritual activity of the West, which also included Monteverdi and Rembrandt. The extract we are presented with—classified under the technical heading of Philosophy, within the general category of the book production of that time—is like a desiccated, anatomical sample. The life that explains it places it back in the midst of

the vital forces by which it was nourished—and which also gave
life to Philippe de Champaigne and Georges de la Tour, Simon
Vouet and the three Le Nain brothers (the oldest being a little
older than Descartes, the two others being a little younger), not
to mention Hardy, Mairet, Rotrou (whose work never quite gets
beyond extravagant tragicomedy), and Desmarets, who published his *Les Visionnaires* the same year as the *Discourse,* just
after Corneille published *Le Cid.*

Furthermore, let us say that the *Discourse* that was read in
1637 by Parisians who had just seen the first performances of
Le Cid and *Les Visionnaires* is (in its true vitality) something
completely different from the *Discourse* that was read by Heinrich Ritter in 1814 (who is of the opinion that one finds "few
new things" in it and that "one can only attribute to Descartes
the merit of having more clearly formulated the generally
widespread way of seeing")—1814 being not only the year in
which Fichte died and Schelling published his *On the Divini-
ties of Samothrace* but also the year in which Géricault painted
The Wounded Cuirassier, probably right as Ritter, still a young
philosopher in Berlin, was enlisting in the army and departing
for the campaign in France. And the *Discourse* is a third thing
still when read by a candidate for the *agrégation de philosophie*
who has just seen the exhibition of tapestries by Le Corbusier
or Preminger's film *The Moon Was Blue.*

This study of contemporaneities (without as yet raising
any questions regarding the direct influences either received
or exerted by philosophy) immediately sheds important light
on the philosophical work that is thereby derigidified, un-
schooled, and revitalized. Even if it were only (and it is actually
much more) a perspectival effect highlighting the life coursing
through the work at the moment of its blossoming, it would
still be interesting to know that Heraclitus's philosophy is contemporary with the temples of Selinunte and Agrigento (those
dramatic conflicts between geometrical proportion and the
human scale); that Saint Thomas Aquinas's *Summa Theolog-
ica* came into being at the same time as the Beauvais Cathe-
dral (that effort to raise the structural ideal of Gothic art to the
greatest scale physically possible, which, in the end, was exe-
cuted perfectly); that Descartes, as we have just recalled, did

not belong to the generation of Le Brun but to that of Georges de La Tour, the painter of *flammulae,* philosophically akin to Descartes through the common influence of Pierre de Bérulle; that the philosopher David Hume and the painter Allan Ramsay were born only two years apart, both in Edinburgh (and one could make a close comparison of their respective studies of human nature); and finally, that the year of Bergson's birth was also that of the poet Albert Samain and of the painter Georges Seurat. It is a human fact that Bergson is chronologically grouped with the Neo-Impressionists and not with Monet, Manet, Sisley, Pissaro, Renoir, and their whole phalanx, who were, on average, twenty years older and well into their careers when Bergson was still a student—and Bergsonism, as a spiritual fact, cannot be uprooted from this fact without damage.

That is why the test of precisely applying, to philosophemes, the aesthetic characteristics of their moment must be granted so much importance. This test allows us to seek not only the total, human significance of the moment but also its dialectical functionality, and thereby to rediscover this functionality in the philosophical work that expresses it in its own way. Our commentaries on Plato grow more fertile when we situate him in relation to the art of his time, as Pierre-Maxime Schuhl has done—when, with Schuhl, we say of Plato's oeuvre that "in Hellenic art of the same period, we find grand masters seeking new ways forward, as well as archaizing tendencies,"[1] and point out "the accord between the Platonic Ideal and the compositional and proportional qualities that mark the new Sikyon school."[2] We say so much about Abelard when we observe, with Ernst Cassirer, that he should be viewed not as a Gothic but as a Romanesque thinker; or, more precisely, that his thought is situated at the exact moment when the great artistic revolution, of which the Basilica of Saint-Denis is the first testament, was under way. And we go quite a ways in our explication of Leibniz when we recall that he is essentially and in his innermost thoughts a Baroque thinker; even further when we recall that the *aesthetic motivations* of his philosophy (and they are extremely important for some of his central ideas) are the very same ones that characterize the Baroque. In this regard, it is enough to recall the themes of "as much variety as possible," and of the subdivision "without end, each part divided into parts having some motion of their own," in §§57–58 and §65 of the *Monadology,* as well as his ideas regarding the symbolization of composites with simples and regarding Expression as a genus of which natural perception, animal sensation, and intellectual knowledge are all equally species *(Letter XXIV to Arnauld),* and so on throughout his work.

Let us hasten to add that, under this first aspect, art is not speculatively privileged. Confronting a philosopheme with its artistic context is only meant to reestablish the integral, intellectual moment and to integrate the philosopheme into that moment. The scientific context, the social and economic contexts are also very important. We should only note that even if this artistic reintegration is not privileged speculatively, it is often privileged methodologically—especially when we are dealing with philosophers (like Plato, Descartes, and Leibniz) who are particularly attentive to their scientific contexts. The artistic confrontation makes particularly clear the kind of "supplement of soul" that raises philosophy above the plane of scientific reflection that serves as its base.

The second order of facts concerns the *paradigmatic importance of art for any given philosophy.*

The preceding facts were of a collective and impersonal nature. In principle, such facts remain independent of any personal knowledge the philosopher might have had of art or of particular works of art. Furthermore, the question of a philosopher's "artistic sources" is quite distinct from the issue with which we were just dealing, especially as these sources often come from a different epoch than the philosopher's own. If Lucretius often made use of sculptural sources and especially of the glyptic art of his time (Adrien Blanchet has pointed out several examples of this), he was not, in any case, dealing with works that had a particularly contemporary character. And the temporal gap can be quite great in other cases. Let us cite a few that spring to mind. For one, August Comte's literary and poetic sources: the enormous influence that Dante's visions had on him is not only apparent in his positive religion but also figured into many pages devoted to his philosophical and sociological speculations—the solidarity between the living and the dead, the static and dynamic faces of collective structures, and so on. And we would certainly misunderstand the effect that music had on Bergson's mind were we simply to say that he reflected on it, that he took it up as a point of comparison, and so forth. Instead, we should say that certain passages from Wagner's music are the sources of certain pages from Bergson. Finally, as regards our contemporaries, if you will permit him to recall it here, the author of the present article noted, some twenty years ago in this same *Revue,* the perfect identity between the essential themes of Heidegger's philosophy and those that lay at the heart of Albrecht Dürer's most celebrated works.

As can be seen, this is not at all a question of superficial examples, serving to illustrate the occasional page of philosophy: we really mean that they are sources. They are all the more important in that they sometimes go unspoken; in that they proceed by impregnation and inspiration; in that they have played a role that has informed the very soul of the philosopher, in its depths and through personal remembrance. Ravaisson's philosophical connection with Leonardo da Vinci's oeuvre so permeated his thought that, in the end, he himself considered it to be something of the order of metensomatic reminiscence. In truth, we could only ever understand such influences sufficiently if the genesis of philosophical vocations were better known to us, and if, in the specific cases in question, we were able to reach back to the origins of the philosopher's *Weltanschauung,* which quite often takes shape well in advance of his professional vocation.

The influence art has—and, more precisely, the influence certain particular works of art have—on the mind of a philosopher is not at all equal from one individual to the next. But in each case where such an influence can be found, it appears to be something private and profound and to be tied to the fact that every key theme that is introduced into a philosophy by the spectral presence of a work of art acts upon that philosophy subterraneously and almost constantly. Its influence can be felt across vast swaths of the entire body of works. For it remains remarkable that the technical explication of the thematic paradigm found in art is still nearly undefined. *Knight, Death, and*

the Devil and *Melencolia I* say more than fifty-some-odd pages
of *Being and Time*: they are fundamental inspirations.

But we would still be far from grasping the philosophical significance of such facts if we were content simply to understand
them as biographical accidents, isolated inspirations, or even
a kind of consultation (however salutary) with art. That would
merely be to sketch the methodological value of a spiritual operation whose overall makeup will only appear through the
systematic and monographic exploration of the philosophical
content of art. When George Santayana reminds us that true
philosophy is found as much among the poets as it is among
professional philosophers and that three poets, Lucretius,
Dante, and Goethe, summarize all of European thought; when
Marcel Brion speaks of "the notion of time in Rembrandt";[3]
when Charles de Tolnay analyzes the philosophical symbolism
of Michelangelo's compositional schemes; when Robert Grin-
nell, Wilhelm Koehler, Erwin Panofsky, Pierre Francastel, and
many others find in the plastic arts and, specifically, in variations of pictorial perspective the historical modifications of a
collective manner of thinking space—all these points of view
and all these works contribute to an idea that is very simple
but loaded with consequences, namely, that besides the philosophy that is verbally expressed in technical works, there is
a spontaneous and living philosophy, expressed in the plastic
arts, in music, or in poetry, that deserves just as much attention
as the technical philosophy we find in books.

But does this then mean that we are dealing with some sort
of diffuse philosophy, existing on the fringes of technical philosophy? Not at all—and that is the important point. If, to the
pure and simple study of simultaneities, we add the study of
correspondences of content, a major fact appears: the almost
constant and often quite significant lead the philosophy contained in art has on professional philosophy. Such symptoms
are sometimes quite difficult to grasp and to translate concep-
tually: it is as if the first rays of dawn were first seen glimmer-
ing upon the summits of art, before then descending into the
depths of the philosophical valley. But is it even necessary to
state that revolutions taking place within human spirit often
emerge clearly and distinctly in the artistic realm well before

the resulting waves can be felt in the domain of philosophy *stricto sensu*? One major example: the Renaissance, the poetic and artistic aspects of which emerged nearly two hundred years before its technical aspects in philosophy.[4] This is how the idea that reflection on art would be the study of the precursors of mind came about.

The third relation (which we can call the *speculative relation*): the place that the philosopher, after reflection, has assigned to meditation upon art within his own philosophy (or within philosophy in general, as he conceives of it). Roughly speaking, and maybe somewhat superficially, this is the philosopher's aesthetics and the place of this aesthetics in the totality of his system.

It should be said that this is often a sort of limitation, which a philosopher assigns, after the fact, to an artistic ascesis he has already endured in a deep and comprehensive manner.

Roughly and somewhat superficially, we said a moment ago. Perhaps also deceptively. In the first place (as follows from the preceding), the explicit aesthetics, with which the philosopher satisfies the need for this speculative relation by making an architectonic decision, is relatively insignificant when compared with the implicit aesthetics that can be teased out through an examination of his works. This operation is often tricky, is sometimes risky, and is always fruitful. Even though it is almost entirely implicit, Descartes's aesthetics has been the specific focus of several works, though not nearly enough.[5] Leibniz's aesthetics has not yet been the specific focus of any satisfactory works. And yet, Leibniz's aesthetics might even be more important than Descartes's, given the profundity of this aspect of his work, as well as the fact that, as we saw a moment ago, it helped to engender many of his metaphysical ideas. We will return shortly to the subject of the influence that Leibniz's aesthetics has had. In the second place, even for philosophers, who—like Kant, Hegel, and so on—have dedicated an entire work to systematic aesthetics, this aesthetics often only responds in part to the problem that has called for its explicit presence. What is most important in Kant's aesthetics is the way in which it is inserted into the system and the organic and functional role that it plays therein; it is the need that Kant felt, at a certain point in his philosophical development, to approach the critique of judgment from an aesthetic angle.

There are still other difficulties we will have to reflect on in our examination of the explicit aesthetics as a specialized organ of the philosopheme. Two such difficulties are of particular importance.

First, it is sometimes the case that this aesthetics is not quite original, that it is either partially or completely borrowed, all while still playing an important organic role.

Bergson made three great contributions to aesthetics: (1) the book on *Laughter,* in which he applied a posteriori certain major themes of his general philosophy to a very specific problem; (2) the numerous pages in his works that address, in passing, though always in a manner intimately tied to the work's spiritual unfolding, problems related to certain arts or to art in general, to aesthetic categories (and especially to Grace), to the particular talent that characterizes the artist, and so on; (3) the magnificent pages, too little known and often overlooked by those who address his aesthetics, where, in the introduction to his scholarly edition of *De natura rerum,* he analyses the aesthetic allure of certain philosophical systems, in particular, the "poetry of atomism."

But it is very important to add that, at first, Bergson adopted an aesthetics that had already been formulated by others— most notably, by Félix Ravaisson, Gabriel Séailles, Jean-Marie Guyau, and others, including especially the adherents of the theory of the *Einfühlung*—and that his conception of intuition promotes the ideas of these aestheticians to the level of a general theory of knowledge.[6] The "received" aesthetics, in Bergson, is perhaps more important as a source of philosophical inspiration than is the "given" aesthetics.

This leads us directly to the second difficulty. Thanks to a prejudice that is, without a doubt, hardly philosophical, but arises frequently enough in those who graze the communal fields of philosophy with a sort of hasty nonchalance, a philosopher who grants a particularly important place in his oeuvre to reflecting on art is immediately labeled as an aesthetician and is thereafter considered to be a specialist, confined to a single philosophical discipline. Sometimes this is the case because one fails to seek out the general philosophy contained within the aesthetics, and sometimes because one considers the aesthetics and the general philosophy, or moral philosophy, and so on, to be two distinct parts of the philosopher's work. Plenty of evidence of such unreflective haste could easily be found in the judgments that have been directed at thinkers like Santayana, Benedetto Croce, and so on. Anyone who is truly a philosopher will sense what an absurdity it would be—and how misrepresentative of actual perspectives it would be—to remove from the dossier concerning the philosophical importance of art only those testimonies that prove to be the most thorough and penetrating to be found on the subject, only to set them aside in a dossier all their own.[7] If we therefore consider aesthetics to be the awareness, on the part of the philosopher, of the relations between his philosophy and art, we must recall that this awareness is sometimes, perhaps even often, imperfect and incomplete.

Let us now turn our attention to the fourth relation: *the philosopheme considered as a work of art.*

This is an aspect of our subject that is quite ancient and persistent, but it is certainly no more simple and straightforward for all that.[8] It has often taken on a polemical guise: if Aristotle ranges Plato's dialogues alongside the epic poems (and not dramatic works); if Destutt de Tracy and Ribot consider, not all of philosophy, but specifically metaphysics to be a work of the poetic imagination; if Renan insists on the impossibility of giving rigorous conceptual methods to philosophy, because of its close kinship with the arts—this is clearly done in a pejorative spirit (and notably with a false notion of the nature of the arts and of the existence of a certain kind of truth in them, namely, the *veritas in essendo*). On the other hand, certain great minds, who need not be suspected of harboring any kind of antiaesthetic bias, have been discomforted by the thought that, on this plane and under this aspect, every fundamental difference between art and philosophy would be abolished. However, this discomfort is excessive, provided it is only a question of philosophy being art under *one* of its aspects, without denying that under other aspects, it can still differ from it fundamentally, or provided there remains a profound difference between philosophy and the other arts.[9]

The main question, then, is to know if, in considering the philosopheme as a work of art, we cast the philosophical approach in an oblique, partial, and almost paradoxical light, making certain details stick out and thereby obscuring what is most important with shadows—or if, on the contrary, we bring something essential to light.

Opinions on this point differ. But it must be said that among those who oppose the idea of presenting philosophy according to its artistic content, some can be called into question straightaway: their arguments rest on prejudices that are hardly philosophical and refuse a frank and clear consideration of the question. For such thinkers (who are thankfully much fewer in number today than they were fifty years ago), the idea of art only evokes something superficial and frivolous—and to such an extent that even the point of view we ask them to consider seems, to them, to be superficial and frivolous, and to lack the profundity and majesty of true philosophical labor. Such thinkers are not entitled to have a say in the matter.

Nor are those who, having only a slight understanding of what art is, judge that such a point of view would immediately rob philosophy of any communication with the idea of truth.[10] No a priori of this kind can be accepted: we must first consider the facts, even if that means we only seek their significance afterward.

More dangerous—because they address the question in a direct, if also limited and insufficient, way—are those who, when confronted with the question of the philosopher's art, can only ever think of matters of style, composition, and presentation, and who even have a tendency, when a philosopher turns out to be rather gifted in this respect, to see this as only having a sort of superfluous value. No one will deny, of course, that the stylistic pains to which a philosopher goes (or does not go!) shed light on that philosopher's temperament and on his philosophical approach. No one will deny that it is difficult to imagine Plato adopting the slack and careless style of Plotinus, or Bergson writing with the ponderous weightiness of Auguste

Comte; or that (as Émile Bréhier has said) Plotinus's style is tied to his theory of philosophical inspiration and Bergson's "images" (see Bréhier again, and also Lydie Adolphe) are not just intimately and functionally related to his entire theory of philosophical thought but even play a methodological role in it.[11] Finally, no one will deny that a philosopheme's influence and its ability or inability to attract minds are inseparable from such questions of expression. Can we really maintain that this aestheticity, which is functional in Bergson, is not so in the case of others or that Bergson's ideas, had they been written clumsily or copied down in an incomplete and non-Bergsonian manner by listeners or disciples (as has been the case for so many philosophical works, from Aristotle to George Herbert Mead), would still retain their fundamental value?

But who can fail to see, with the work of any philosopher whatsoever, that we are in the realm of art, or rather that art is in the philosophy itself? Art *is* the philosophy itself, inasmuch as we are concerned with (1) the gradual unfolding of its fulfillment, (2) its architectonic organization, (3) its accomplishment in an interhuman, spiritual presence—in short, with the *anaphor* of all that this philosophy *is.* And this is true whether we want to view this philosophy as an organic ensemble of ideas, or as the shared expression of an intuition of reality, or even as a mode of existence or a mode of action, so long as its fundamental vection is always leading to a work, and that work would actually be the philosopher himself, insofar as he has been instaured by his philosophy.

And it would be vain to object that this is not art but life. Beyond the spiritual level with which we are dealing here, any distinction between art and life is abstract and artificial; and in this domain, it will prove to be the case that art is a principle lying at the heart of life, not the other way around. Only a non-instaurative philosophy (but would it even be a philosophy in that case?) could claim not to be an act of art—for art is nothing but the wisdom of instauration.

That is why anyone who hopes to explain the philosopheme while omitting the instaurative wisdom from which it proceeds, which animates and accomplishes it, will only ever put forth a "system" (in the most pejorative sense the term can be

given). And even in such a system, even if crystallized and scle-
rosed, the crudest effects and most obvious motivations of that
artistic principle, from which it has, as a work, resulted, will still
subsist.

To be sure, it is necessary to take fully into account the noble
misgivings of those who want to ensure that, in addition to the
veritas in essendo that organizes it, the philosophical work also
has a *veritas in cognoscendo,* which may not be univocal between art and, for example, scientific knowledge. But this latter truth is related to its contents: it is based upon the contents
of the philosopheme, whether those are properly scientific or
experiential and even vital. Moreover, this is a condition that
differentiates the philosophical art from all the other arts as
soon as reference is made to a mode of methodological knowledge that is independent of art. But does the philosophical mo-
bilization of every knowledge that is the object of a legitimate
agreement come about in any other way than in relation to
this *veritas in essendo,* without which there would be no philosophical accomplishment? And it is easy to see that even the
question of legitimate agreement itself only makes sense if it is
reexamined in light of the philosophical end and subordinated
to it. How, for instance, could we account for the law of philosophical destruction, which destroys, in every philosopheme,
a significant portion of the knowledge that common—or even
philosophical—experience had previously taken to be accepted, if it were not an act of thought organized in relation to
the truth of being? Let us not then say that philosophy "adds"
this truth, which lies at the heart of art and relates to the philosophical whole, to another truth that had previously been
seen in the details (though that might be sufficient to satisfy
the aforementioned misgivings). Instead, let us observe that
the act of art that animates and accomplishes the act of philosophizing always takes it upon itself to revise the prior agree-
ments borrowed from disciplines other than philosophy itself.
And it is up to each particular philosophy to decide up to what
point it will make use of this right to destructive revision. Some
philosophies use it only ever so slightly. None abstain from it
altogether. And the principle of this revision is at once distinctly
philosophical and essentially artistic. It is often asked if it is le-

gitimate for the philosopher *to choose* which facts he takes and which he leaves, which he grants a privileged status and which he takes to be secondary. In reality, the philosopher does not choose: the choice is inherent in the anaphoric experience, which places the facts in an architectonic situation within the philosopheme. And that, too, is art. Let us not forget that art is a veritable ontological experience: an exploration of the paths that lead a cosmos from chaos all the way up to its accomplishment in patuity.

The fifth and final relation to consider (and it will bring us back from essential, pure art to the specialized activities of the fine arts) is the *life of philosophy in art.* This is what one might somewhat strictly call the influence of philosophy on art. It might seem that this is a point of view that would only be of interest to the art historian—and yet it should also be of the greatest interest to the historian of philosophy.

To know that philosophy cannot be isolated, that it must endeavor to mobilize, assemble, and thetically express the entire situation of thought at a given moment, and that every piece of human evidence that moment has to offer is of value to it, is not only to ask it to embrace and unify art, science, and the practical activities of that particular human moment but also to ask it for something other than some sort of total, or even ultimate, result. It is to want it to be not only clarifying but vitalizing and animating. That the spiritual form (I take this word in its Blakean sense), that the spiritual form of a philosopheme, I say, should be a directive and generative force is itself a proof of its truth (in the same sense as when this truth was defined earlier). That is why observing the development of a philosopheme through mankind's activities—whether all of them or only a few more specialized ones—allows us to explore not only its vitality but also its authenticity, inasmuch as it is a perspective on the more or less distant future of mankind.

Thus, for example, certain philosophies have provoked an aesthetic ferment when still fresh and novel, which they were subsequently unable to sustain: after this initial filtration, their destinies could only be pursued elsewhere. Epicureanism, which, so soon after its birth, found and inspired a poet of genius, would never subsequently find such an artistic audience again (among the minor French libertine poets of the seventeenth century, who did refer to Epicureanism, the only great poet was La Fontaine, and he only turned to it for a handful of moral themes, drawing largely on other sources for his poetic inspiration). At various times, however, and especially in the nineteenth century, Epicureanism did play a powerful, if largely unspoken, role in the development of the scientific mindset. As for Stoicism, which at first was so rich in aesthetic elements, the only great human discoveries it has led to have been in the juridical and institutional realms. On the other hand, there are certain doctrines from antiquity whose impact across time has been immense from an aesthetic point of view. Aristotelianism, for instance, is not technically an aesthetic philosophy (and the influence of its aesthetics is almost entirely limited to the effect the *Poetics* had on the French theater of the seventeenth century) but a logical, moral, and metaphysical one. And yet, even though it has often been presented, perhaps excessively, as having hindered the development of science during the Middle Ages, it had a long and fertile influence upon the poetry and architecture of that age.[12] But since then, its influence has been more restricted, without, however, dying out altogether.[13] Only two ancient philosophies have had artistic destinies that were both grandiose and perennial: in the first place, Pythagoreanism (not only through its immense and direct influence on music but also in the form of neo-Pythagoreanism, which is present everywhere in da Vinci, influenced Dürer up until the final renunciation expressed in *Melancholia,* and is again currently exercising a strong influence, mixed with Platonic elements). And then there is Platonism, whose artistic vitality has never wavered, though its great triumph was certainly the Florentine Renaissance. A philosopher will fail to grasp the historical probity and philosophical breadth of the Platonic vision if he forgets Ghiberti, Botticelli (his whole oeuvre, not just *Pallas and the Centaur*), and Michelangelo (at least as far as the architectonic of his compositions is concerned), which is to say, if he forgets what makes the history of Platonism a living reality. Need we elaborate with still more facts of this kind? Let us limit ourselves to recalling that if the Baroque Leibniz, of whom we spoke a moment ago, had no influence on the art of his day, the pre-Romantic elements of his philosophy (the theory of *petites perceptions*; the dynamic conception of expression; the fact that, for the monad, "everything must arise for it from its own depths"[14]) resurfaced with the publication of his posthumous works and made a strong impact on Goethe and Herder—and, through them, on all of Romanticism. Let us also recall that if Proust denied having any debt to Bergson, Péguy and other writers (like Jean Paulhan) have openly recognized their debts to him.[15] Let us not forget the professed philosophical sources of Surrealism. And let us recall that Freudianism (which should be considered to be a general philosophy) has had a profound effect on the literature of the present age, as well as on cinematographic art, on drawing, and especially on engraving (and this fact is symptomatic of the realization that this philosophy is more graphic than plastic).[16]

Thus, the serious question of the temporal significance of works of art (which gave Karl Marx so much trouble) is rediscovered in the question of the temporal significance of philosophies: and a philosophy's continued vitality in the sphere of the arts is certainly the best touchstone we have at our disposal in this regard. But this is no coincidence: the force of aesthetic animation contained in a philosophy is inherent in its innermost being as a spiritual form.

Now, perhaps, having gathered all of this together, we will be permitted to conclude. Some of these conclusions will concern art and will serve, in particular, as a reminder (which is always useful) of the scope and effectiveness of its spiritual mission, not to mention its power to probe into the future.

But what we are most interested in showing concerns philosophy.

In the first place, from a practical point of view, perhaps it would not be unimportant to remind philosophy of the scope of its vocation, which is to say, of the fact that it ought to accept all the expressions of the spontaneous, spiritual activity of mankind—of which art is one of the most important and best established. If the author of these lines may be permitted to offer a few personal reflections, a fortunate evolution has taken place in this regard since the time already long past (some twenty-five years now) when, in setting forth some of the ideas

and facts that have been brought together here, he encoun-
tered a certain amount of incredulity in the philosophical cir-
cles, which, at that time, were still too convinced of an almost
scholastic twofold primacy, among the parts making up the
art of philosophizing, of reflection on science and of the history of philosophy. To be sure, we have come a long way since
then. And the majority of the considerations we have thought
to bring together here to seek their architectonic will no longer
seem paradoxical to the reader of today, who will certainly recall having heard one or another of them either expressed or
challenged (and with much more talent than here) by various
contemporary thinkers.

But perhaps a holistic point of view will emerge from this
architectonic assembly—and what better fruit could we hope
for it to yield?

The existence of five major relations between philosophy
and art, all distinct and yet each existing organically in an in-
timate union with the others, constitutes something like the
successive interplay of various perspectives, which allows us to
see something hidden in the depths. Perhaps we are not saying
enough when we insist upon a common, instaurative vection,
which would be of a total, human significance and would be
like the common framework for the expressions, whether philosophical or artistic, of the human anaphor.

It may not be enough, but it is already saying a lot: it is con-
firming and encouraging philosophy in the instaurative vocation of which it loses sight and maybe even loses altogether
when it limits itself either to enumerating and (dare we say) fid-
dling with prior acquisitions, or to scholasticizing these acquisitions dogmatically without looking further into the future—
all while the more impatient arts, in which there is still some
youth and life to be found, go beyond and seek something new.
Philosophical inventiveness, which is so restricted in comparison with artistic inventiveness (Nietzsche's "Embark, philosophers!" is always more relevant than philosophers concede), is
held back at every moment by philosophy's tendency to want
to follow its own groove, especially when the groove is freshly
cut. The lively audacity with which art frees itself from its own
track might, up to a certain point, be a lesson for philosophi-

cal thought. For too few philosophers practice the Pythagorean maxim of avoiding the beaten path. In philosophy, whoever walks off the beaten path, the path that has clearly been trod by the greatest number in that generation, is too often considered not only to be unusual, and therefore lacking in authority, but to be something like a latecomer, when, in reality, since he does not walk where οἱ πολλοί *(hoi polloí)* walk, he has forged ahead. The example of art (where it is almost always loners, exploring the *avia loca,* who have the greatest hold on the future) could encourage philosophy to pay greater attention to the symptoms, not of the contemporary, but of the more or less distant future—and precisely that is one of its missions. Whoever considers matters in this way will see his perspective shift, and not fruitlessly.[17]

But I said it is not enough. That philosophy should be instaurative (like and with art) we do not doubt. But what does it hope to instaur?

Initially, it is awareness of the present moment in its human totality, with all its riches, all its deficiencies, all its aporias, and all its aspirations, even when they are contradictory. But, from there, it is not enough for it to seek the new and inventive acquisition, which will go beyond these aporias—for that, art would be enough. It must assume a responsibility that does not belong to art, namely, that of the total and truly anaphoric promotion, which coordinates the present moment with the future in accordance with a hierarchy.

Art progresses by the perpetual enrichment of the Pleroma of works, such that every Young Wisdom (as the Gnostics said) could be welcomed into the Pleroma and recognized as a new aspect of the eternal wisdom—provided it found in its moment the conditions for its temporal insertion.

While philosophy does also progress through the arrival of new philosophemes, enriching the Pleroma, this is not what distinguishes it from the other arts. Its difference lies in the fact that it demands from each new instauration a promotion, an advancement of the totality of the Pleroma according to an order that is certainly not temporal but to which time must be able to acquiesce in order for the progress also to be a progress for man in his real existence.

Now, here, too, the process remains profoundly tied to art, since it is through art that, note after note, the melody is accomplished, without any note that has already sounded being a matter of indifference, and without any note that sounds having its value derive from itself alone but only from the accomplishment. Saying that the authentically philosophical progress accomplishes humanity would perhaps be enough if we had a sufficient notion of the immense demand involved in the word *accomplish*. And perhaps that is the principal demand and the great responsibility of philosophy. Yet no philosopheme is sufficient unto itself. A "philosophy of philosophies"—only judicatory in what concerns philosophical accomplishment—is indispensably engaged, albeit implicitly, in the progress of the Great Work, if only to the extent that it works to instaur a new point of view that would be able to transcend each individual intuition of the philosopher in his particular situation. And the anaphor of this point of view in the particular works that can contribute to it constitutes the harmonic framework of the μεγίστη μουσιχή *(megístē mousichḗ)*. To correct his personal point of view, or a "collective point of view," in order to make it an element of the total harmony in which humanity is accomplished in its futurity (and certainly in relation to its own existential status of transnaturality) is to recognize himself as and make himself a cooperative part of the μεγίστη μουσιχή *(megístē mousichḗ)*. To refuse this personal ascesis and still to claim to philosophize is to push philosophy back toward the status of being one art among others. But the ambition to make philosophy the supreme art is the key to true philosophical efficacy, for anything capable of guaranteeing the success of this ambition does not just observe but really brings about the accomplishment of the Great Work, at the level of existence of the Pleroma.

Notes

1. One Monad Too Many?

1. Fernando Pessoa, *The Book of Disquiet,* trans. Margaret Jull Costa (New York: New Directions, 2017), 266: "Living seems to me a metaphysical mistake on the part of matter."
2. Pessoa, 18.
3. Pessoa, 235–37.
4. Pessoa, 237.
5. Pessoa, 235. Cf. Souriau's remark in "La conscience," *Quaderni della "Biblioteca filosofica di Torino"* 17, no. 4 (1966): 574: "What man, being no more than a man, would dare to claim that he thinks in such a way that he therefore exists indubitably? Therein lies Descartes' error."
6. For a more complete bibliography of Souriau's works, cf. *Dictionnaire des philosophes,* dir. D. Huisman (Paris: Presses universitaires de France, 1993). [All translations from Souriau's works are my own. For all other sources, when possible, I have attempted to use the most current English translations available to me; if no published translation is cited, the translation is my own. —TN]
7. In IP, Souriau defines philosophy as a "'pure art' of thought" (147) and asks "what, in the philosophical works of the last thirty years, makes it so that some of these works are, for instance, related more to Debussy than to Ravel,

or more to Monet and Manet than to Derain, Vlaminck, and Matisse, or more to Horta and Otto Wagner than to Bruno Taut and Le Corbusier, and so on" (143). See also the article "Art et philosophie," *Revue philosophique de la France et de l'Étranger* 144 (1954) [translated as "Art and Philosophy" and included as an appendix at the end of this volume], in which Souriau invokes both an explicit aesthetics, which would be a systematic "part" of a philosophy, and an implicit aesthetics, which profoundly animates the architectonics of the philosophical work. "Let us not forget that art is a veritable ontological experience: an exploration of the paths that lead a cosmos from nothingness to its accomplishment in patuity."

8. DME, 187: "Existence is all the existences, it is each mode of existing. It resides and accomplishes itself integrally in them all, in each taken on its own." This statement echoes an earlier one: "For art is all the arts. And existence is each of the modes of existence. Each mode is an art of existing unto itself" (DME, 131).

9. IP, 367: "Existing is always existing in some manner. Having discovered a manner of existing, a special, singular, new, and original manner of existing, is existing in your own manner."

10. AA, 94. Also 113–14: "These lucid points, these pure bursts of light would have to be regarded a little like mountain peaks in dawn's light . . . ; peaks that are made to appear, here and there in a mountainous region, by a pink haze at the sublime hour. But this pink haze itself would have to be regarded as a kind of illumination all its own, an *Alpenglühen,* a luminous palpitation which would be the direct reality itself and, as such, would not so much draw these peaks forth from the shadows where they would otherwise exist in some somnolent state, but would install and instaur them. For this splendor would be their very being."

11. In certain texts, Souriau seems to conceive of his existential pluralism on the model of the diversity of the arts (see, e.g., DME, 183), but he goes on to correct this, to show that a deeper art exists: "it would not seem strange

to look for [the solution] in the vicinity of something that participates in art, rather than in any other instaurative path that would be fit for providing it with some sort of model—on the condition that it be sufficiently expanded and grasped in its pure principle—a generic art or pure art of existing common to those different arts of existing, of which we must choose and practice one if we are to have existence" (DME, 184).

12. [The French term *fond* (and related terms, such as *fonder, fondement*) is translated here as "ground" (and its variants) to highlight the connection Lapoujade draws between Souriau's existential pluralism and the philosophical problem of grounding. While I do primarily stay with the language of "grounding" throughout, I sometimes turn to alternate translations, such as "foundation" or "establish" (which map onto the language of Souriau's philosophy of *instauration* quite well), as context demands. For more on the problem of grounding, cf. Gilles Deleuze's *What Is Grounding?* [*Qu'est-ce que fonder?*], trans. Arjen Kleinherenbrink (Grand Rapids, Mich.: New Centre for Research and Practice, 2015). —TN]

13. Martin Heidegger, *The Principle of Reason,* trans. Reginald Lilly (Bloomington: Indiana University Press, 1991), 51: "Ground/reason is missing from being. Ground/reason remains at a remove from being. Being "is" the abyss in the sense of such a remaining-apart of reason from being. To the extent that being as such grounds, it remains groundless."

14. Souriau, "La conscience," art. cit., 577. He borrows this expression from Jules de Strada's *Ultimum Organum* (Paris: Hachette, 1865), 288.

15. On the notion of the "pluriverse," cf. "The One and the Many," Lecture IV of William James's 1907 *Pragmatism* lectures, in *Pragmatism and Other Writings* (New York: Penguin Classics, 2000), 58ff.

16. *Patuity,* another term borrowed from the *Ultimum Organum* of philosopher Jules de Strada (1821–1902), designates the fact of being apparent, the "quality of being apparent by virtue of being just what it is." Souriau also

makes use of the Latin term *patefit,* which designates, not the quality, but the event of being apparent.

17.　Souriau invokes a "monadology of philosophemes" (IP, 267). On the divergence: "Our starting point must be the *divergence* of philosophies, which grow farther and farther apart to the extent that they push their world . . . toward its perfection in terms of both determination and existence. No postulate will allow us to eliminate this divergence, for it is *real* in philosophical thought" (IP, 214).

18.　IP, 63: "This gesture, by which all these reflections or acts are transported to a distinct and entirely spiritual world, established or re-established there, and, in the end, posited individually in being—*that* is the philosophical gesture *par excellence*" (see also IP, 229, 235–36).

19.　AA, 86: "The only means we are presented with is to study the problem . . . in the domain of certain special presences, which, on the one hand, do not correspond to anything objective, and yet, on the other, only register in our souls because they are actually more organized and determinate than their initial subjective presences would make it seem: vaguely formed from a sketch barely begun, honed from a more or less enigmatic intentionality."

20.　[While the French term *personnage* will be translated as "character" in the context of, say, a discussion of a Platonic dialogue or a novel (cf. especially chapter 3), it will be translated primarily as "persona" in most other contexts, to retain the allusion to the "conceptual personae" *(personnages conceptuelles)* of Deleuze and Guattari. —TN]

21.　Gilles Deleuze and Félix Guattari, *What Is Philosophy?,* trans. Hugh Tomlinson and Graham Burchell (New York: Columbia University Press, 1994), 70–73.

22.　René Descartes, *Discourse on the Method,* part III, in *The Philosophical Writings of Descartes,* vol. 1, ed. John Cottingham, Robert Stoothoff, and Dugald Murdoch (Cambridge: Cambridge University Press, 1985), 125.

23.　Franz Kafka, "Letter to His Father," in *The Sons,* trans. Ernst Kaiser and Eithne Wilkins (New York: Schocken Books, 1989), 152.

24. Franz Kafka, *Diaries, 1910–1913,* trans. Joseph Kresh (New York: Schocken Books, 1948), 28.

2. Modes of Existence

1. On the pure *patefit,* OD, 101–2, where the description Souriau gives of pure existence—"It is thus"—is fairly close to the descriptions of "firstness" we get in Peirce. Cf. Charles S. Peirce, *Écrits sur le signe,* trans. Gérard Deledalle (Paris: Seuil, 1978), 83–84. [Cf. *The Collected Papers of Charles Sanders Peirce* (Cambridge, Mass.: Harvard University Press, 1931–35), 1.304, "Qualities of Feeling." —TN]

2. DME, 133: "Initially manifest, the phenomenon thus becomes manifestation."

3. DME, 147: "As this *réique* status implies, thought is purely and simply liaison and communication" [translation modified].

4. DME, 146: "*Réique* existence is constituted by thought, and yet thought itself is constituted, resides, and operates in *réique* existence, as well."

5. DME, 147–48: "All that we affirm of psyches, in noting that they belong to this same mode of existing, is that they have a sort of monumentality that makes of their organization and form the law of a permanence, of an identity. Far from compromising the life of the soul by conceiving of it in this way, we would fail it to a much greater extent if we did not conceive of the soul as an architectonic, as a harmonic system susceptible to modifications, enlargements, occasional corruptions, and even wounds . . ." [translation modified].

6. DME, 147: "Let us speak more generally of an ontic mode of existence that will be suited to psyches and also to *réismes.*"

7. DME, 154: "Their essential characteristic is always that the magnitude of the intensity of our attention or concern is the basis . . . the bulwark upon which we erect them; without there being any other conditions of reality than that."

8.   Souriau stresses that the intensity of the affects consti-
     tutes "the polygon of sustentation of their monument"
     (DME, 154).

9.   DME, 153: "Therefore, just as there are imaginaries,
     there are also (if we dare say) emotionals, pragmatics,
     attentionals; whatever is important in such and such a
     care or such and such a qualm; in short, a *solicitudinary*
     existence."

10. Henry James, *The Art of the Novel: Critical Prefaces* (New
     York: Scribner's, 1934), 119–21.

11. Souriau makes it clear that his inventory of the modes of
     existence is arbitrary and contingent (DME, 182).

12. Regarding negation, we could compare this with the "neg-
     ative prehensions" in Whitehead. Cf. Alfred North White-
     head, *Process and Reality* (New York: Free Press, 1978),
     220–21, and Didier Debaise's analysis in *Speculative Em-
     piricism: Revisiting Whitehead,* trans. Tomas Weber (Ed-
     inburgh: Edinburgh University Press, 2017), 73–75. This
     is equally true in the domain of individual existences:
     "We will observe that these virtual beings, whose out-
     lines have been limned by the play of events and cosmic
     propositions, and whose multiplicity or scale enrich our
     souls merely in being proposed, even before they are re-
     alized, are far from all being equal as regards moral value.
     Among them we also find the Incompatibilities, the Un-
     playable Roles, the Temptations, the Fallen Self: so many
     themes of accomplishment which we can rightly refuse
     to accomplish; without, however, thereby preventing this
     halo of virtualities from surrounding us" (AA, 63).

13. IP, 337: "In a philosopheme, there are certain positive
     zones of affirmation and of clear and nearly unilateral in-
     stauration; and then certain zones where there reign cor-
     relative facts of positive affirmation and of deliberate and
     existential negation: This is not! It is a phantom that will
     not survive the right light."

14. James, *Art of the Novel,* 120.

15. AA, 60–61: "There is something in the factual order,
     something all around us, which poses the problem of our
     greatest existence. And we ourselves . . . , when we feel

a sort of need to grow mentally and to install ourselves on a level of substantial greatness completely different than our current one, we only exist as such through ambition—through an ambition that is sometimes justified and sometimes not. It is a problem to be solved. To be clear: this is not a theoretical problem to be solved by a philosopher engaged in speculative study. It is a concrete problem actually needing to be solved for the person who tries, through appeals of the kind we just mentioned, to exist a greater and more substantial existence than the one in which he now feels himself to be insufficient."

3. How to See

1. Cf. *Brancusi vs. United States: The Historic Trial, 1928,* trans. Nina Bogin and Kirk McElhearn (Paris: Adam Biro, 1999), 124: "The artist must grasp the spirit of nature and attempt to create a world exactly like the creation of nature: forms that affirm their right to life" [translation modified]. Cf. also Bernard Edelman, *L'Adieu aux arts: Rapport sur l'affaire Brancusi* (Paris: L'Herne, 2011), and Céline Delavaux and Marie-Hélène Vignes, *Les Procès de l'art* (Paris: Palette . . . , 2013). It is surprising that Souriau wasn't more occupied with the legal domain, considering its penchant for the modal transformation of existences. In each case, the general question is, what is the mode of existence (and who is its owner)?

2. Or again, AA, 62: "As far as the self is concerned, because it is theoretically implicated in certain phenomena, [phenomenology] tends to suppose that it really is a part of their reality, and to reconstitute it as if it were always anterior and even exterior to the phenomena that imply it (first the self in the world, then the self outside the world)." See certain remarks made by Husserl, for instance, *Ideas for a Pure Phenomenology and Phenomenological Philosophy, First Book: General Introduction to Pure Phenomenology,* trans. Daniel O. Dahlstrom (Indianapolis, Ind.: Hackett, 2014), §49, 90: "The entire spatiotemporal world (to which the human being and the human ego are to be

reckoned as subordinate individual realities) is, *in terms of its sense, a merely intentional being,* that is to say, the sort of being that has the merely secondary, relative sense of being *for* a consciousness."

3. DME, 136, where Souriau wants "to actually carry out the existential reduction that is the exact antithesis of the phenomenological reduction" and "make the pure phenomenon the center of [the] entire systematics . . . [since] that is what it would be to place ourselves in the point of view of the phenomenon."

4. See, for example, what Souriau says of philosophy: "By writing, the philosopher wanted . . . to present people with an objective means by which they could show themselves certain things in a certain way. He constructed this monument for them, committed it to writing, and placed it in their midst" (IP, 34–35).

5. Also: "Its beginning is the pure—and, so to speak, still dumb—psychological experience, which must now be made to utter its own sense with no adulteration." Husserl, *Cartesian Meditations: An Introduction to Phenomenology,* trans. Dorion Cairns (New York: Kluwer Academic, 1999), 38–39.

6. See, for example, William James's essay "Does 'Consciousness' Exist?," in *Essays in Radical Empiricism and "A Pluralistic Universe"* (New York: E. P. Dutton, 1971), 3–4.

7. David Hume, *An Enquiry Concerning Human Understanding* (Indianapolis, Ind.: Hackett, 1993), section IV, part I, 17: "Adam . . . could not have inferred from the fluidity, and transparency of water, that it would suffocate him, or from the light and warmth of the fire, that it would consume him."

8. In each philosophy's point of view, Souriau sees an ideal persona: "an ideal and interior witness, which the work introduces so that it may be established in relation to it; and with which every soul, coming into contact with the work, will have to identify to a greater or lesser extent."

9. Henri Bergson, *Matter and Memory,* trans. N. M. Paul and W. S. Palmer (New York: Zone Books, 2005), 10: "We place ourselves at the point of view of a mind unaware of

the disputes between philosophers." On the operation of the reduction in *Matter and Memory*, cf. Camille Riquier, *Annales bergsoniennes* (Paris: Presses universitaires de France, 2004), 2:261–62.

10. Cf. James, *Art of the Novel*, 214: "They are splendid for experience, the multiplications, each in its way an intensifier." Cf., also, on the subject of *What Maisie Knew*, 148–49: "the 'mixing-up' of a child with anything unpleasant confessed itself an aggravation of the unpleasantness."

11. Regarding her "grids," Agnes Martin even invokes a state of innocence: "When I first made a grid I happened to be thinking of the innocence of trees and then this grid came into my mind and I thought it represented innocence, and I still do, and so I painted it and then I was satisfied. I thought, this is my vision." Cited in Frances Morris's *Agnes Martin: Innocence and Experience* (London: Tate Modern/DAP, 2015), 56.

12. On the importance of material, and its recuperation and recycling in contemporary art, cf. Tristan Manco's *Raw + Material = Art: Found, Scavenged and Upcycled* (London: Thames and Hudson, 2012). In philosophy, it is William James who defines the domain of "pure experience" as a "material" (or "stuff"), which he distinguishes from mere matter.

13. Jean Dubuffet, *Prospectus et tous écrits suivants*, tome III (Paris: Gallimard, 1995), 100, and tome I (Paris: Gallimard, 1967), 56.

14. Cf. Michel Tournier, *Friday; or, The Other Island*, trans. Norman Denny (New York: Pantheon, 1985), and Deleuze's analysis in *The Logic of Sense* (New York: Columbia University Press, 1990), 301–2. Each of these authors has an interest in the Robinsonade that goes back quite far, as can be seen in Tournier's "L'impersonnalisme," *Espace* 1 (1945), and in Deleuze's "Desert Islands," in *Desert Islands and Other Texts* (New York: Semiotext(e), 2004), 9–10.

15. Olivier Cadiot, *Future, Former, Fugitive*, trans. Cole Swensen (New York: Roof Books, 2003). If "Zero sum"—as Cadiot uses it—refers to game theory, it also refers to a cogito reduced to zero by the vertiginous proliferation

of possibilities that traverse it and are mixed up in it. Cf. what Cadiot says of Robinson in *Les Temps modernes* (Paris: Gallimard, 2013), no. 676, 17: "He is an artist or a saint without knowing it. He has all the qualities, but none sufficiently complete for him really to become anything. . . . His desire for perfection makes him extremely versatile—he is a transformist: we watch as he changes his perspective, morphing continuously, because he radically identifies with his projects."

16.   G. W. Leibniz, *Discourse on Metaphysics,* in *Philosophical Essays,* trans. Roger Ariew and Daniel Garber (Indianapolis, Ind.: Hackett, 1989), §9, 42: "Thus the universe is in some way multiplied as many times as there are substances." Cf. also DME, 102–3.

17.   If zero is the point of conversion, what happens beneath the degree zero? At "Less than Zero"? In *Less than Zero,* and in Bret Easton Ellis's other novels, we are dealing with characters in search of a threshold beyond which they would be able to perceive or be moved, but they never get there. In a certain sense, they aren't even characters, since they don't show us anything but render everything indifferent and equal. Perceptions and emotions remain superficial, like all the rest. They never become truly profound, which is to say, they never transform what is perceived, no matter what the shock that prompted them might have been (for instance, the screening of the snuff film or the voyeuristic prostitution scene in *Less than Zero*). Even drugs don't change perception; they are merely ordinary, social accoutrements, like champagne. It is like writing, which is "blank" in a way, distant from everything, with blank characters, emotionally blank, blank from the coke, blank from their inability to feel anything at all (even the imperceptible suffering this inability gives rise to), blank from having become strangers to all. "People are afraid to merge on freeways in Los Angeles." It is a shared world, though one in which nothing is shared but for agreed upon signs of social recognition—a world and stories without perspective.

18.   It is Deleuze who, following Tarde, made "having" a char-

acteristic of the Leibnizian monad in *The Fold: Leibniz and the Baroque,* trans. Tom Conley (Minneapolis: University of Minnesota Press, 1993), 107–8. Leibniz's influence is particularly apparent in *L'Instauration philosophique,* where, despite his critiques of Leibniz, Souriau presents the history of philosophy as a vast monadology (IP, 267, 383).

4. Distentio animi

1. Souriau, "Of the Mode of Existence of the Work to-Be-Made," in DME, 220. Cf. also the article "La conscience," where Souriau opposes this hypothesis to the obviousness and clarity with which the Cartesian *cogito* is given.

2. DME, 172: "Just as the phenomenon is, in certain respects, a sufficient and indubitable presence, with which we would be able, if necessary, to construct an entire universe . . . ; so the event is an absolute of experience, indubitable and *sui generis,* with which we are also able to make an entire universe, perhaps the very same as that of the ontic, though with an entirely different existential poise."

3. Jorge Luis Borges, "Tlön, Uqbar, Orbis Tertius," in *Labyrinths,* trans. James E. Irby (New York: New Directions, 1964), 8.

4. [*Le fait du fait.* For the sake of the text's readability, I have translated this phrase simply as "the fact of the fact"— even though this translation obscures the relationship between *le fait* (the fact) and the verb *faire* (to do), of which *fait* is the past participle. In *The Different Modes of Existence,* I sometimes translated *le fait* as "the 'what-is-done,'" to highlight the verbality of "the fact," which is so crucial to Souriau's discussion of the event (cf. chapter 3, section 3). Lapoujade's use of "the fact" throughout this paragraph should be understood to include this sense, developing the distinction between "the 'what-is-done'" and "the fact of the 'what-is-done.'" —TN]

5. Souriau dedicated an article to the notion of the instant, in which he defined life as "the organization of these

instants, which are rationally posterior to their very being."
Cf. *Les Études philosophiques* 2, no. 2/3 (1928): 96–102.

6. "For example, an instant only truly exists if all of the
    virtual content with which it is supposedly charged, ef-
    fectively attains an expression that is sufficient both for
    the the right to be and for an abundant, pointed kind of
    existence." Cf. "Le hasard, les équilibres cosmiques et les
    perfections singulières," *Les Études philosophiques* 15,
    no. 1/2 (1941): 14.

7. Cf. also AA, 38: "The extent of a soul's perspective grows
    with its states of need, its desires, its feelings of dissatis-
    faction; each of these things is one of its dimensions."

8. OD, 101: "In all of its continuances, in all of its subsequent
    echoes, it will always remain . . . that which it can no lon-
    ger not have been."

9. AA, 131. Cf. "The harmonic contrast between two struc-
    turally dominant, psychic themes instaurs and measures
    a distension of the soul and outlines an interior grandeur
    on the axis of this architectonic opposition" (AA, 131).

10. Marguerite Duras, *Writing*, trans. Mark Polizzotti (Minne-
    apolis: University of Minnesota Press, 2011), 28–29.

11. François Roustang, *Influence* (Paris: Minuit, 1990), coll.
    "Critique," 175.

12. It is Dubuffet who speaks of matter's "poignant move-
    ments" and "intimate urges" in *Prospectus et tous écrits
    suivants*, tome III, 101. Among authors fascinated by the
    mineral, we might think of Roger Caillois, or of Pierre
    Gascar, who, in his strange tale *L'Arche* (Paris: Gallimard,
    1971), is fascinated by the secret lives of caves, their milky,
    opalescent world, which is "illuminated by a flat light that
    doesn't shine." Gascar makes thought communicate with
    an inhuman world that plunges it into a deep night, a
    dream before dreams giving rise to lightless forms, akin
    to the blind, diaphanous animals that populate these
    caves. This fascination is inseparable from an exclusion
    from the human world, from "states of moral destitution
    and solitude so great . . . they force upon you a feeling of
    kinship with the walls."

13. Souriau: "Even form itself is not without explanation. It

engenders itself. Its presence is always the radiant solution to a problem; it is the summation of the spiritual exigencies leading to the upheaval of a being." "Sur les moyens et la portée d'une esthétique de la grâce," *Revue de métaphysique et de morale* 43, no. 2 (1936): 298.

14. Souriau takes up the scholastic distinction between beings that exist through themselves (aseity—from *a se*) and beings that exist through another (abaleity—from *ab alio*). Cf. AA, 6 and DME, 158.

15. Henri Bergson, "Dreams," in *Mind-Energy*, trans. H. Wildon Carr (New York: Henry Holt, 1920): 117.

16. Bergson, 118.

17. On the vampirism of memory that puts an end to the vitalism of *Creative Evolution*, cf. Camille Riquier, *Archéology de Bergson* (Paris: Presses universitaires de France, 2009), 359–60.

18. So, for example, on the subject of consciousness, in "La conscience," 575: "First ideal of consciousness: lucidity. And this ideal is intensive."

19. DME, 188: "[We have] had to compare unimodal identity to a sort of curvature of the plane of existence, curled or crumpled in such a way that what is separate on the plane makes contact with itself and interpenetrates, integrates into a single ontic existence. But here it would be a matter of bending two planes of existence, of bringing them into contact with one another and making them interpenetrate, such that a single being occupies a place in both at once." Cf. also DME, 129–30.

20. DME, 129: "[But] this rising existence is ultimately made up of a coinciding, double modality in the unity of a single being, which is progressively *invented* over the course of the labor. Often without any foresight: up to a certain point, the resultant work is always a novelty, a discovery, a surprise. *So this is what I was looking for, what I was destined to do!* Joy or deception, compensation or punishment for attempts or errors, for efforts, for true or false judgments."

21. See the analysis of this example by Isabelle Stengers and Bruno Latour, DME, 15–17.

22.   DME, 236: "In every realization, whatever it may be, there
       is always a measure of failure." Cf., for example, Giacom-
       etti's remarks in *Alberto Giacometti* (Paris: Musée d'Art
       Moderne de la Ville de Paris, 1991), 415: "I know that it is
       completely impossible for me to sculpt, paint, or draw a
       head, for example, a head like I see before me—and yet it
       is the only thing I ever try to do. Whatever I'm able to do
       will only ever be a pale image of what I see and my suc-
       cesses will always, at bottom, be failures and perhaps no
       more than failures."

23.   DME, 237: "Let us not confuse the evidence of the com-
       pletion with the work's finish, or with the stylistics of what
       are commonly, or in the terms of industry or commerce,
       referred to as 'finishing touches.' A crude confusion to
       which the artists of certain epochs, whose sketches or
       drafts are better than the finished works, have at times
       succumbed." Cf. also IP, 355–56.

5. Of Instauration

1.   See, for example, the lecture "Roman et réalité" in Nath-
      alie Sarraute, *Œuvres complètes* (Paris: Gallimard, 1996),
      1643–44.

2.   Eugène Dupréel, *Essais pluralistes* (Paris: Presses univer-
      sitaires de France, 1949), 257. Now forgotten, the Belgian
      philosopher Dupréel (1879–1967) is the central figure of
      what is known as the Brussels School. His most important
      works deal with the notions of convention, consolidation,
      and interval.

3.   Dupréel clearly insists on this point, since it is a question
      of finding, "in the convention, the characteristics of what
      is retained as *formal*. The convention is a form or a system
      of forms, something distinct from and relatively indepen-
      dent of the continuous collection of actions, objects, and
      circumstances to which we find it joined. A philosophy
      that gives the notion of convention an explanatory power
      in relation fundamental questions is a *formalism*" (14).

4.   Dupréel, 257 and 251: "The most remarkable thing this
      process presents to its investigator is the production of

something new. There is, in the consequent, a contribution that is irreducible to the antecedent."

5. OD, 42: "True philosophy is, *at the very least,* instauration, in that it must create the point of view from which the living, concrete, and varied totality we take responsibility for can be grasped in an architectonic unity."

6. IP, 402: "And such is the originary Anarchy: the fact that all singular accomplishments can be considered, in isolation, as primary (in the sense that the Cartesian *cogito* is primary, as can be shown without any further questioning). But they all have the cosmic demand within them, from the fact of the relational network they outline and from the manner in which they mutually limit each other. Also, in isolation, they can only have a weak, initial degree of existence. That is why, all together (and, as it were, chorally), they demand the accomplishment of the cosmos, as the pleroma of singular existences."

7. IP, 310: "My point of view, which is to say, the point of view that defines me, and not a point of view that originates in me, since I would be nothing without everything in which I am constituted and consolidated myself."

8. IP, 390: "If the reader really wanted to follow our slightly puerile, but structural fable . . ."

9. IP, 263: The heightening of the reality and complexity of a cosmos demands "a drop in the potential of the virtual riches belonging to a content that is thereby set on the course of determination."

10. On this point, cf. Michel Serres, *Le Système de Leibniz et ses modèles mathématiques* (Paris: Presses universitaires de France, 1968), 665f.

11. For a detailed presentation of these laws, cf. Fleur Courtois-l'Heureux's article "Le philosophème et ses lois d'instauration," in the collective volume *Étienne Souriau, Une ontologie de l'instauration* (Paris: Vrin, 2015), 87–110. Cf. also Souriau's rearticulation of these laws in relation to the musical laws of harmony in the article "Sur les moyens et la portée d'une esthétique de la grâce," art. cit., 298. Determination is pure sound as tonic; opposition is the dominant; mediation is the major or minor

third; and evasion is the appoggiatura as the "aberrant element."

12.   In *Chercher une phrase* (Paris: Bourgois, 1991), Pierre Alféri sketches a theory of literary instauration fairly close to Souriau, which he opposes to the philosophical logic of grounding: "The instauring gesture takes the form of a retrograde step. But the retrospection here is not a foundation; the origin it attains is not a grounding. A grounding is discovered retrospectively over the course of an examination. . . . It is an anterior absolute. . . . In literature, retrospection is active and instaurative in itself" (14).

13.   IP, 229: "Regarding these gestures, one thing is certain: the greater a philosophical thought is, the more simple its gestures will be—grand acts that eliminate a universe still lost in particulate confusion and present it successively, stroke after stroke, with new forms for determining and structuring it. Grand, informing gestures." Further on, Souriau describes the philosophical categories as "gestures of thought" (IP, 297).

14.   James, *Art of the Novel,* 224. Or again: "I am so put together as often to find more life in situations obscure and subject to interpretation than in the gross rattle of the foreground." "The Beldonald Holbein," in *Complete Stories, 1898–1910* (Boone, Iowa: Library of America, 1996), 393. [Souriau cites Tzvetan Todorov's introduction to *Nouvelles,* Aubier-Flammarion, 1969, p. 16. —TN] Cf. also Souriau: "We know the extent to which daily existence—in those moments that are most difficult to bear and most effectively rid us of the desire to live—is dull and lacking in depth, intimacy, and internal echoes. All at once, the poetic experience opens up what was thus closed, flat, and superficial and fractures it into the thousand responses being makes to itself, with all its voices superimposed and in concert with one another." "Le langage poétique comme fait interpsychique," in *Poésie et langage* (Brussels: Maison du poète, 1954), 208.

15.   IP, 365, on the subject of philosophy: "Having achieved its completion, it is an absolute. The kind of witnessing that

it involves is an essential witnessing; a formal place into which anyone may settle." Cf. also IP, 9.

16. Cf. IP, 240: "It is always a vast ensemble, cosmic in nature, that is made to appear in being oriented around a more or less clear point, which one might call testimonial. This testimonial point can serve to designate and to name concretely a point of view."

17. DME, "On the Mode of Existence of the Work to-Be-Made," 235.

18. Hugo von Hofmannsthal, *Hugo von Hofmannsthal and the Austrian Idea: Selected Essays and Addresses, 1906–1927*, ed. and trans. David S. Luft (West Lafayette, Ind.: Purdue University Press, 2011), 35; and, on the present age, 37: "A mild, chronic dizziness vibrates within it. There is a great deal in it that has been made known only to a few, and much that is not there, although many believe that it is. So the poets might well ask themselves from time to time whether they are there, whether for their epoch they are somehow really there."

19. Hofmannsthal, 41, and 43–44: "He is unable to regard anything in the world and between the worlds as off limits. . . . Yes, he is unable to pass by even the most conspicuous thing."

20. Hofmannsthal, *The Letters of the Man Who Returned*, in *Writings on Art/Schriften zur Kunst*, ed. Hans-Günther Schwarz and Norman R. Diffey, trans. Marlo Burks (Munich: Iudicium, 2017), 2:64.

21. Hofmannsthal, 84.

22. Hofmannsthal, 92.

23. Hofmannsthal, 96.

24. Souriau, "Le hasard, les équilibres cosmiques et les perfections singulières," art. cit., 15.

6. The Dispossessed

1. Kafka, *Diaries*, 28.

2. Kafka, "Letter to His Father," 161: "Why then did I not marry? There were certainly obstacles, as there always

are, but then, life consists in confronting such obstacles. The essential obstacle, however, which is, unfortunately, independent of the individual case, is that obviously I am mentally incapable of marrying."

3. Kafka, 121.

4. Kafka, 152.

5. Kafka, 122. Every little thought he had "[was] from the beginning burdened with [the] belittling judgements" of his despotic father, so his already "hesitant, stammering mode of speech" ended in silence. "The impossibility of getting on calmly together had one more result, actually a very natural one: I lost the capacity to talk" (126). In *Diaries*, 25: "The bachelor, however, has nothing before him and therefore nothing behind him. At the moment there is no difference, but the bachelor has only the moment." See also, later in *Diaries*, 169: "he, this bachelor, still in the midst of life, apparently of his own free will resigns himself to an even smaller space, and when he dies the coffin is exactly right for him."

6. Elias Canetti, *Kafka's Other Trial: The Letters to Felice*, trans. Christopher Middleton (New York: Schocken Books, 1974), which finds in Kafka's letters to Felice a trial that runs parallel to the composition of *The Trial*. Cf. 70: "He is cognizant of the fact that he is conducting his trial against himself; nobody else is fit to conduct it."

7. Franz Kafka, *Letters to Milena*, trans. Philip Boehm (New York: Schocken Books, 1990), 63.

8. Franz Kafka, *The Trial*, trans. Breon Mitchell (New York: Schocken Books, 1998), 160.

9. Kafka, "Letter to His Father," 142.

10. Samuel Beckett, *Waiting for Godot*, in *Samuel Beckett: The Grove Centenary Edition*, vol. 3, *The Dramatic Works* (New York: Grove Press, 2006), 13.

11. Samuel Beckett, *Fizzles*, 4, in *Samuel Beckett: The Grove Centenary Edition*, vol. 4, *Poems, Short Fiction, Criticism* (New York: Grove Press, 2006), 410.

12. Cf. Samuel Beckett, *The End*, in *Poems, Short Fiction, Criticism*, 289—the comic scene between the political orator and a character who doesn't understand what the other

wants from him: "Take a good look at this living corpse. You may say it's his own fault. Ask him if it's his own fault. The voice, Ask him yourself. Then he bent forward and took me to task. I had perfected my board."

13. Samuel Beckett, *Malone Dies,* in *Samuel Beckett: The Grove Centenary Edition,* vol. 2, *Novels* (New York: Grove Press, 2006), 173.

14. Cf. Beckett, *Fizzles,* 8, 418–20.

15. Samuel Beckett, *A Piece of Monologue,* in *Dramatic Works,* 454.

16. See, for example, Bill Viola's statement about cameras: "These machines are keepers of the souls; they capture souls." Remarks collected by Christian Lund, Louisiana Museum of Modern Art in London, 2011.

17. James Pritchett, *The Music of John Cage* (Cambridge: Cambridge University Press, 1993), 59. [Cited from Cage's 1948 autobiographical lecture "A Composer's Confessions." —TN] We might also think of the experience, at the origin of *4'33",* Cage had in a perfectly soundproofed room at Harvard University, where, in spite of everything, he still heard the high-pitched sound of his nervous system and the deeper tones of his blood's circulation.

18. Interview with Pierre Encrevé, *Beaux-Arts Magazine,* Hors-série 1996, "Les éclats du noir," 54.

19. Agnes Martin, in Morris, *Agnes Martin,* 124.

20. On Agnes Martin's "classicism," cf. Rosalind Krauss, *Bachelors* (Cambridge, Mass.: MIT Press, 1999), 75–76.

21. On this point, Henri Maldiney, *Regard Parole Espace* (Lausanne, Switzerland: L'Âge d'homme, 1973), 183–84.

22. On methods close to this in cinema, cf. Gilles Deleuze, *Cinema 1: The Movement-Image,* trans. Hugh Tomlinson and Barbara Habberjam (Minneapolis: University of Minnesota Press, 1986), 84–86.

23. Cf. the interview on http://www.art21.org/: "If I look at some white panels in my studio, I see the white—but I am not conscious of them being white. They react with the wood, the color, the light and with the wall itself."

24. Remarks recorded in 1964 by Calvin Tomkins in *The Bride and The Bachelors* (New York: Viking Press, 1965), 203.

25. "L'intérêt esthétique," *Lire: Revue d'esthétique* 2/3,
     no. 10/18 (1976): 20. [Cf. 27n4: "*Pregnancy.* Allow me to
     note that I take this word, here and always, in its etymo-
     logical sense and not in the sense in which it is techni-
     cally employed in the theory of forms. This latter sense
     traces back to the German *Prägnanz*, which itself in-
     volves a significant semantic distortion with respect to
     etymology: it would be best translated as *concision,* and
     prägnant/prégnant as *concise.* But, in Latin, *praegnans*
     means *fecund* or *ready to produce.* (Indeed, the term is
     used in the French of physiologists: a pregnant female.)
     When Leibniz said 'the present is big with the future,' he
     might also have said 'pregnant with the future.' As for
     myself, by *pregnancy,* I understand: rich with implicit
     virtualities." Cf. also "Le langage poétique comme fait in-
     terpsychique," art. cit., 208, where Souriau describes po-
     etic experience as "Pregnant Existence." —TN]

Appendix

1. Pierre-Maxime Schuhl, *Platon et l'art de son temps,* 2nd
    ed. (Paris: Presses universitaires de France, 1952), 20.
2. R. G. Steven, cited by Schuhl.
3. We could also cite Georges Poulet's fine *Studies in Human
    Time* here, though they are less to the point, since they
    analyze not only poets (cf. the chapter "Notes on Racin-
    ian Time," as well as the chapters on Vigny, Gautier, and
    Baudelaire) but also philosophers (Montaigne, Descartes,
    Jean-Jacques Rousseau, Diderot). Studies of human time
    in painting, sculpture, or architecture would bear even
    greater fruit. (On the presence and importance of time
    in these arts, the author permits himself to refer you to
    his essay "Time in the Plastic Arts," *Journal of Aesthetics
    and Art Criticism,* June 1949, which deals with the differ-
    ent conceptions of time in Tintoretto, Raphael, Poussin,
    Rembrandt, and Delacroix, as well as differences between
    Egyptian and Greek temples, Romanesque and Gothic
    churches, etc.)
4. At first glance, there is one serious exception to this: Ro-

manticism, of which the philosophical moment that is most often referred to—Fichte, Schelling, Hegel—seems to be inserted between pre-Romanticism and the great literary, pictorial, and musical Romanticism. But whoever truly reflects upon this will see that the three Romantic philosophers only set forth a very limited part of artistic Romanticism and that a certain segment of contemporary philosophy is renewing some of the contents of artistic Romanticism, which was, itself, rather quickly exhausted due to a sort of rapid overexertion of major themes. One benefit of the philosophical analysis of art is that we learn to view things in depth, without being taken in by the apparent simplicity of linear evolutions. Furthermore, the major importance of contemporary neo-Hegelianism is enough to indicate how important the current resurgence of Romanticism has been. It would also be interesting to note—even if it is just a detail—that if we consider Albrecht Dürer to be an important source for contemporary philosophy, it is easy to see that this is due to the ways in which he was viewed, reconsidered, and taken up as a master by the Romantics ("Oh my master, Albrecht Dürer, oh old, pensive painter," etc., etc.). Likewise, the importance granted to the unconscious and to the work of dreams is, as Albert Béguin has shown, a characteristic of Romantic invention.

5.   An old and now nearly useless book by Émile Krantz; a few pages from Lanson; a good article that is a little too condensed by Olivier Revault d'Allonnes; Jean Laporte's unpublished project, intended to be added as a chapter to his *Rationalism de Descartes*; and a page, here and there, in a work of literary history or in an edition of some work or other by Descartes.

6.   Dominique Parodi, for example, has convincingly shown how much Bergson's general philosophy owes to the aesthetics of Gabriel Séailles.

7.   The same prejudice has sometimes also arisen in relation to moral philosophy. A number of histories of philosophy (since Heinrich Ritter, to whom we referred earlier) regularly and almost perfunctorily present the moral

component of a philosophical system last, as if it were no
more than a sort of prolongation, intended to establish,
by way of conclusion, a relation with action. And even
though, for fifty years now, a great number of thinkers
have worked to return considerations based on the reflective study of action to their rightful place (which is often
the principal place), the prejudice to the contrary persists.
Yet we systematically wrong philosophemes if we address
their aesthetics or moral philosophies as if they belonged
to categories that were designated a priori, instead of
seeking the place, in each particular philosophy, where
aesthetic or moral considerations organically take hold.
To grasp the importance of the kinds of research omitted
by such prejudices, it suffices to note how outdated we
now find the attitude, characteristic of so many historians
of the nineteenth century, that consists in systematically
granting primary importance to the theory of knowledge.

8. There is no question of listing every thinker who has spoken of the philosopheme as a work of art. Let us merely
highlight the following, either for having made a singular contribution to the subject or for having discerned an
original aspect of it: Aristotle in relation to Plato, Plotinus,
Maimonides, Destutt de Tracy, Schelling, Renan, Ribot,
Höffding, Édouard Le Roy, Max Dessoir, Paul Valéry, Alain,
Charles Lalo, and, in a recent communication to the Société française de Philosophie, Irwin Edman.

9. In the final analysis, this is Plato's attitude: for him, philosophy is art (and if we forget this, it becomes very difficult
to account for the relationship between the ascending and
descending dialectics, as well as the principle that makes
the latter effective). But it is the supreme art: φιλοσοφία
μεγίστη μουσιχή *(philosophía megístē mousichḗ)*. And this
hierarchy is what is important. Poetry, in particular, is
condemned, not as μουσιχή *(mousichḗ)*, but for being the
art that, by its very nature, impinges upon philosophy's
supremacy and tends to contest its authority.

10. Among those we presented earlier as having pejoratively
used the idea that metaphysics has an affinity with poetry, the principal argument is to make metaphysics into

a work of the imagination and to imply the traditional idea that imagination is "the mistress of error." This theory is as false when it is applied to art as it is when it is applied to philosophy. We should praise Nietzsche for having spoken eloquently of the role of the imagination in philosophy.

11. Even if there were no other reason to link Bergson's philosophy with its expression, the sole fact that, as Lydie Adolphe recalls in *La dialectique des images chez Bergson* (Paris: Presses universitaires de France, 1951), 182, the Bergsonian starting point is "the conception that philosophical problems have been falsified by language" would be enough to show that the care Bergson took to put his thought into language, without it being thereby falsified, was central to his thought itself.

12. Regarding poetry, think of the influence the *Nicomachean Ethics* had on Arabic poetry, on one hand, and on Occitan poetry, on the other. As regards architecture, the morphology of Gothic architecture, those syllogisms in stone, has clear Aristotelian characteristics.

13. From this point of view, there is a significant exaggeration in Jacques Maritain's efforts to Aristotelianize, by way of Thomism, certain daring forms of art and literature that emerged in the first half of the twentieth century. Jean Cocteau's purported Thomism (*bos siculus super tectum*, said Lionel Landry) is probably nothing more than a clever theory about a poet whose only affiliation is Pythagorean, as anyone who has seen his signature would know.

14. [Leibniz, "A New System of Nature," in *Philosophical Essays*, ed. and trans. Roger Ariew and Daniel Garber (Indianapolis, Ind.: Hackett, 1989), 143. —TN]

15. In the end, it must be admitted that Bergson had a fairly small influence on the arts. Perhaps this is because he owed so much to the arts himself and especially to certain art forms that were already on the verge of being exhausted. If the affinity between Seurat and Bergson really can be maintained (despite certain Pythagorico-Platonic elements in Seurat), Cézanne and the Constructivists had

already achieved their greatest pictorial successes by the time the philosophical and literary vogue of Bergsonism grew to its full stature.

16. Here, as in the rest of the work, we have deliberately made use only of major examples. If we had sought more specialized examples (which might appear to be more philosophical or instructive) from philosophers, however unusual they might be, in whose works we find an "aesthetic overdetermination" (Paracelsus, Robert Fludd, Pierre Hyacinthe Azaïs, Jules de Strada, Marcello Fabri, etc., etc.), our work would be less substantial and less convincing.

17. It will be said, "But in philosophy's past, it was not the loners who made their mark but those who were involved in the gradual development of ideas." In the first place, this is a historical error, due to a retrospective interpretation. Next, it would be more than an error or a mistake to reduce philosophical progress to a question of success in the eyes of a public, even a learned public: the search for such success has often been a hindrance in philosophy. And finally and above all, it is precisely the slow, trawling nature of philosophical attention and the lack of vivacity in its rhythms that explain a fact few philosophers would consent to acknowledge: the real and grave lack of major works of philosophical literature, beside an enormous production of minor or insignificant works. This fact is concealed again, in part, by historical distance and also, in particular, by the destruction in antiquity of a number of minor works (or the failure to republish them in the Middle Ages), the loss of many of which will forever be regrettable. The number of works of art is clearly on a different scale than the number of philosophical works. But, to reestablish the equilibrium, we must not forget that philosophical maturation is much slower than the maturation of the works of the fine arts.

David Lapoujade is professor of philosophy at Université Paris 1, Panthéon–Sorbonne, and author of numerous books, including *Powers of Time: Versions of Bergson* (Univocal/ Minnesota, 2018) as well as *Aberrant Movements: The Philosophy of Gilles Deleuze* and *William James: Empiricism and Pragmatism*.

Étienne Souriau (1892–1979) was a French philosopher known primarily in his lifetime for his work in aesthetics. He was a founding editor of the *Revue d'esthétique*, was elected to the Académie des sciences morales et politiques in 1958, and oversaw the creation of the monumental *Vocabulaire d'esthétique* (published posthumously in 1990). He is author of *The Different Modes of Existence* (Univocal/Minnesota, 2015).

Erik Beranek is a doctoral candidate in philosophy at DePaul University. He is translator of Jacques Rancière's *Béla Tarr, the Time After* and Étienne Souriau's *The Different Modes of Existence* as well as cotranslator of *Intolerable: Writings from Michel Foucault and the Prisons Information Group (1970–1980)*, all from the University of Minnesota Press.